CARTOONS and Cartooning

Harvey Weiss

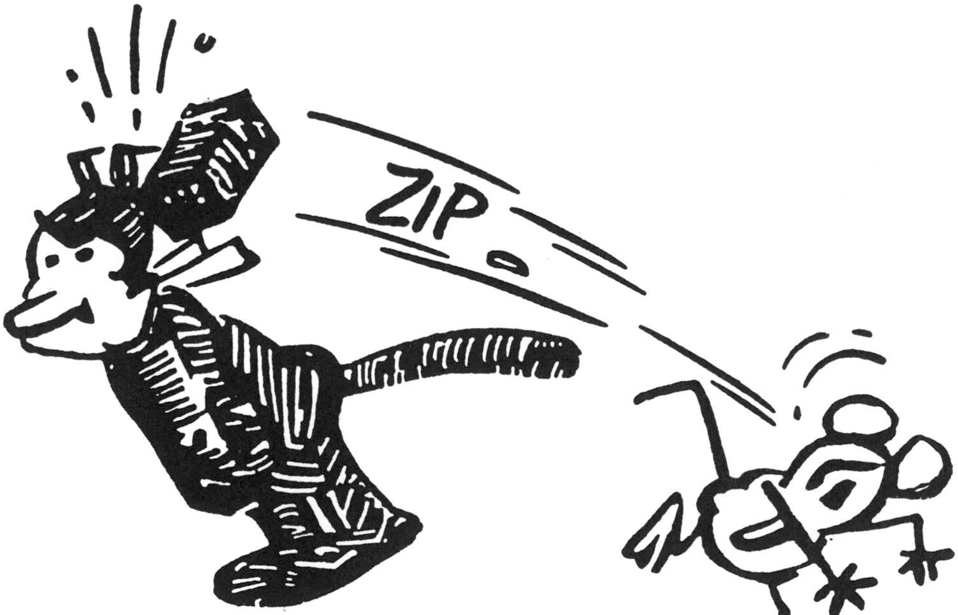
ZIP

Houghton Mifflin Company Boston 1990

Library of Congress Cataloging-in-Publication Data

Weiss, Harvey.
  Cartoons and cartooning / by Harvey Weiss.
      p.   cm.
  Includes bibliographical references.
  Summary: Discusses the many kinds of cartoons—funny ones,
political and editorial ones, caricatures, comic strips and books,
gag panels, animated movie cartoons—and gives hints to the budding
cartoonist.
  ISBN 0-395-49217-3
  1. Cartooning—Juvenile literature.   2. Caricatures and cartoons—
Themes, motives—Juvenile literature.   3. Comic books, strips,
etc.—Themes, motives—Juvenile literature.   [1. Cartooning.
2. Cartoons and comics.]   I. Title.
NC1320.W47   1990   89-39596
741.5—dc20   CIP
                         AC

Printed in the United States of America

P 10 9 8 7 6 5 4 3 2 1

CONTENTS

ACKNOWLEDGMENTS: The author wishes to thank Howard Munce, Walter Einsel, Mel Casson, Jack O'Hara, and Sidney Harris for their assistance and generous permission to reproduce their work. Thanks are also due the Marvel Comics Group for allowing the reproduction of the drawings of John Byrne. Sherman Krisher, former curator of the Museum of Cartoon Art in Portchester, New York, has also been of great help.

The author is indebted to King Features Syndicate for cartoons which are credited throughout the book. All are reprinted with special permission of King Features Syndicate, Inc. *Barnaby*, by Crockett Johnson, is reproduced by permission of Ruth Krauss.

Illustrations not identified in the text are by the following artists: Walter Einsel, p. 8 (drawing in margin), p. 20 (bottom), p. 41 (top), p. 44; Howard Munce, p. 23 (bottom), p. 33 (top), p. 38 (right); Mel Casson, p. 19, p. 33 (bottom), p. 34 (top), p. 41 (bottom left); Jack O'Hara, p. 37 (right), p. 38 (bottom), p. 41 (bottom right); Joseph Low, p. 40 (Mother Goose); William Staples, p. 24 (top). Illustrations that are not credited here or in the text are by the author.

INTRODUCTION

A cartoon can be many things, but basically, it is a way to say something with words and pictures. In most cases words and pictures are equally important, though there are times when the picture alone is used.

Many people think that cartoons are only comic strips — like *Peanuts* or *Little Orphan Annie* or *Blondie*. Not so. Cartoons are of many different types. A cartoon can be funny. It can tell a story. It can give an opinion about something. It can be a beautifully drawn picture — or a simple, scrawl-like sketch. Some cartoons show just one funny situation or illustrate a joke. Others have familiar characters in dramatic stories that go on and on, year after year. There are the comic books. And there are still other kinds of cartoons. This book will take a look at all types.

A good way to start is with some of the cartoons that appeared a long time ago and that, in fact, may not seem like cartoons at all.

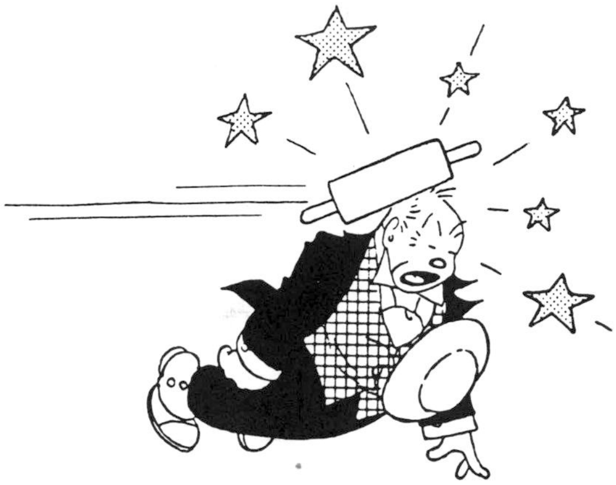

CARTOONS FROM LONG AGO

Cartoons produced years ago often seem strange to us because the style of drawing is different — and the sense of humor is often different, too. There was a great deal of falling down and getting knocked about and sometimes rather cruel goings-on. There was a lot of slapstick. Not many of these cartoons dealt with everyday life and real people.

Whatever the style of the cartoon, the drawing was always good. It was as skilled and carefully done as in the best cartoons of today. Maybe even better. The cartoonists were all well-trained artists.

These early cartoons were mostly individual pictures with a few lines of text underneath. They appeared in newspapers and magazines and were printed in black and white. Many early cartoons were humorous exaggerations, or caricatures. A good way to attack someone you don't like is to make him look silly. And this is exactly what a caricature can do.

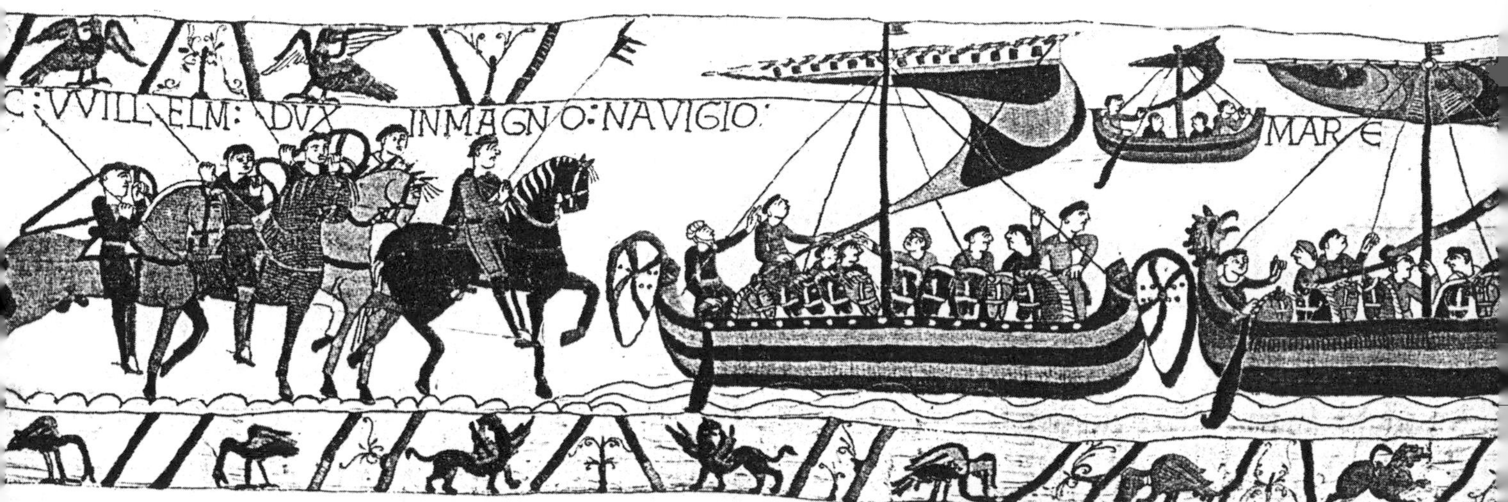
VVILLELM: DVX
INMAGNO:NAVIGIO:
MARE

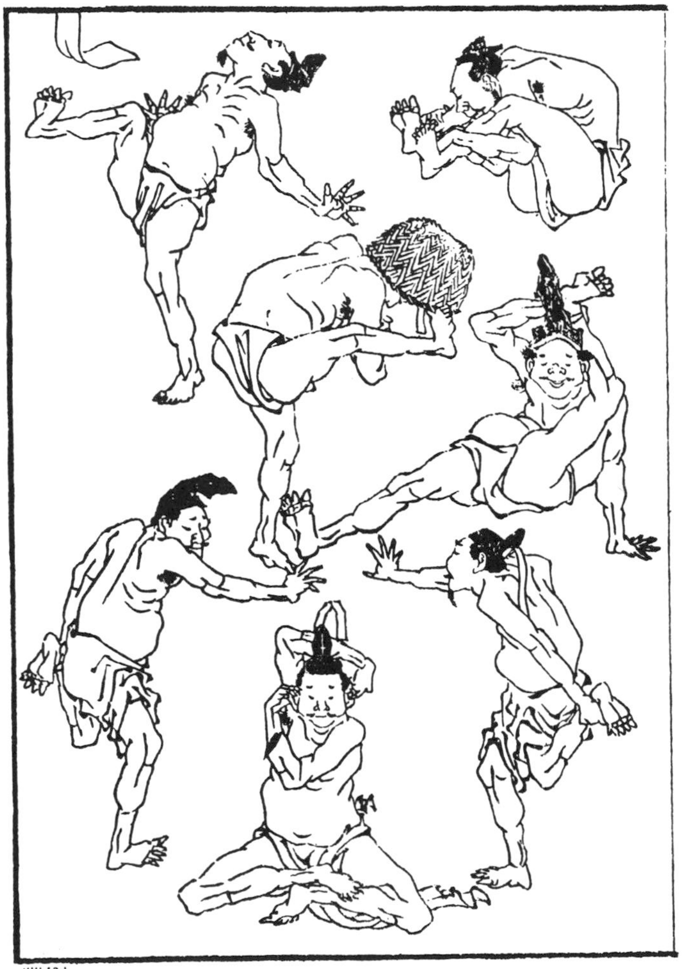

VIII-12-L

This drawing, made in the early 1800s, is by a famous Japanese artist, Katsushika Hokusai. The seven acrobats warming up for a performance are so lively and so funny looking that we can call this a cartoon even though it isn't anything like the kind of thing you might see in a newspaper or a magazine or a comic book.◄

Even though this doesn't look much like an ordinary cartoon strip it really is because it tells a story by means of a sequence of words and pictures — and that is what a cartoon strip does.

What is shown in this strip is the story of the Norman invasion of England in 1066 under William the Conqueror. The figures, horses, boats, and words are embroidered on a linen background 20 inches wide and 230 feet long. The drawing is done not with ink or pencil but with thread.

It was made for the town of Bayeux in France and is called the Bayeux tapestry. The short section reproduced here shows Duke William leading his army down to the ships and setting sail for England.

This must certainly be the longest and most unusual cartoon strip ever made.▼

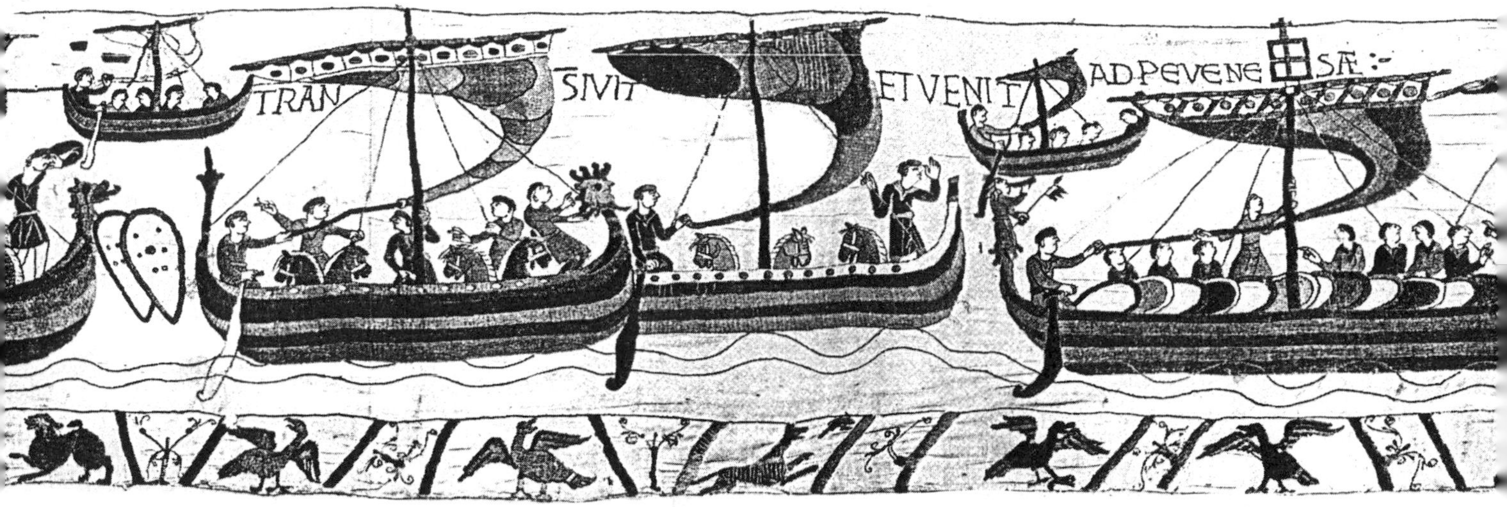
TRAN SIVIT ET VENIT AD PEVENESÆ

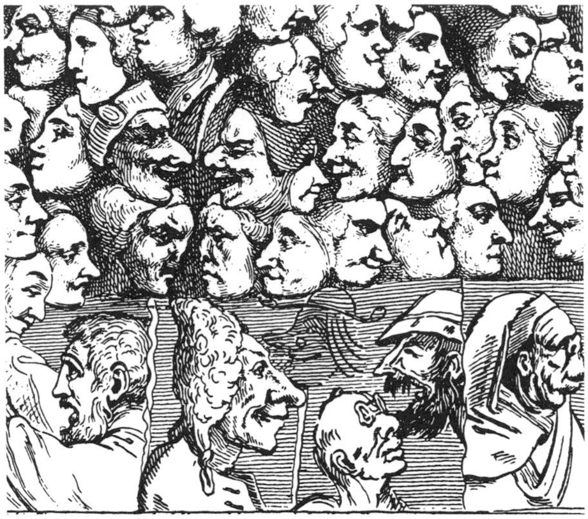

This is an engraving by William Hogarth done in 1743. It shows a variety of heads — some fairly realistic and some caricatured.

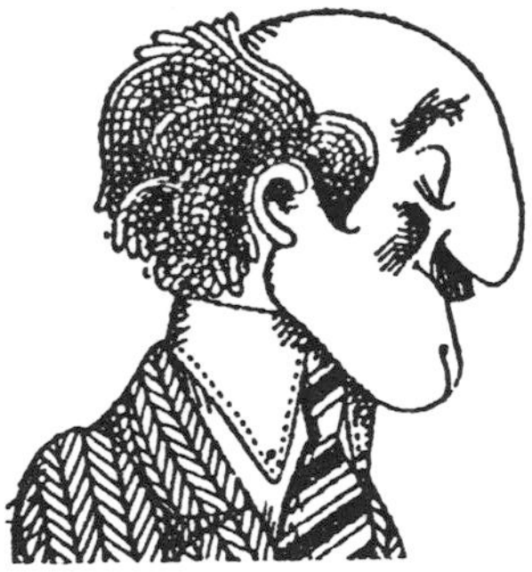

Some caricatures are just funny drawings of heads — not aimed at any particular person. The drawing by William Hogarth is like this. The people drawn by Hokusai in strange poses are also drawn with humor, not in any attempt to make them look bad.

Cartoonists were not always held in high regard. Their work often appeared in lowbrow newspapers in an effort to increase circulation. Some of the better educated and more snobbish readers looked down at what they considered a "common folk" art form. They thought comics were for children and the uneducated. What nerve! This is certainly not the general opinion now. Today comic strips are considered a kind of writing-illustration that has its own special style and character. No other art form is like it, and some very serious university professors write scholarly books about it and study it as a modern art form.

Tens of millions of people of all ages all over the world every day read the comics that appear in their daily papers. And some

In the early 1900s a cartoonist named Winsor McCay produced a series of highly imaginative, beautifully drawn comics called *Little Nemo in Slumberland*. Little Nemo would have some of the wildest dreams — like getting carried away by a walking bed, as in the episode shown here. But after the strangest and most fantastic adventures he would always wake up in his own bed. Half the time, though, he would have fallen out of it and his parents would come running in to see what had happened.►

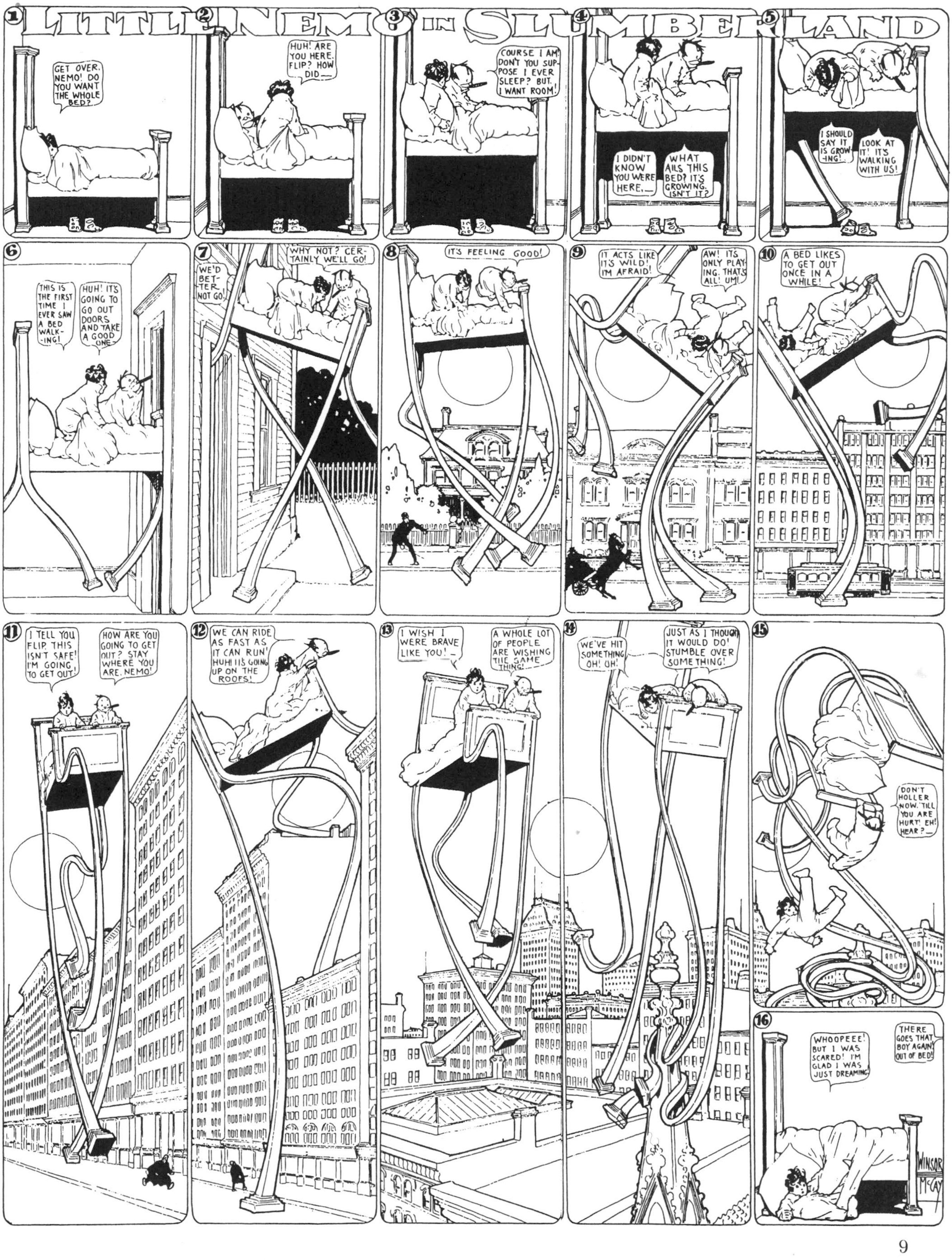
LITTLE NEMO IN SLUMBERLAND
GET OVER, NEMO! DO YOU WANT THE WHOLE BED?
HUH! ARE YOU HERE, FLIP? HOW DID___
COURSE I AM! DON'T YOU SUPPOSE I EVER SLEEP? BUT, I WANT ROOM!
I DIDN'T KNOW YOU WERE HERE,___
WHAT AILS THIS BED? IT'S GROWING, ISN'T IT?
I SHOULD SAY IT IS GROW-ING!
LOOK AT IT! IT'S WALKING WITH US!
THIS IS THE FIRST TIME I EVER SAW A BED WALK-ING!
HUH! IT'S GOING TO GO OUT DOORS AND TAKE A GOOD ONE
WE'D BET-TER NOT GO!
WHY NOT? CER-TAINLY WE'LL GO!
IT'S FEELING GOOD!
IT ACTS LIKE IT'S WILD! I'M AFRAID!
AW! IT'S ONLY PLAY-ING, THAT'S ALL! UM!
A BED LIKES TO GET OUT ONCE IN A WHILE!
I TELL YOU FLIP, THIS ISN'T SAFE! I'M GOING TO GET OUT!
HOW ARE YOU GOING TO GET OUT? STAY WHERE YOU ARE, NEMO!
WE CAN RIDE AS FAST AS IT CAN RUN! HUH! IT'S GOING UP ON THE ROOFS!
I WISH I WERE BRAVE LIKE YOU!
A WHOLE LOT OF PEOPLE ARE WISHING THE SAME THING!
WE'VE HIT SOMETHING OH! OH!
JUST AS I THOUGHT IT WOULD DO! STUMBLE OVER SOMETHING!
DON'T HOLLER NOW, 'TILL YOU ARE HURT! EH! HEAR?
WHOOPEEE! BUT I WAS SCARED! I'M GLAD I WAS JUST DREAMING
THERE GOES THAT BOY AGAIN OUT OF BED!
WINSOR McCAY

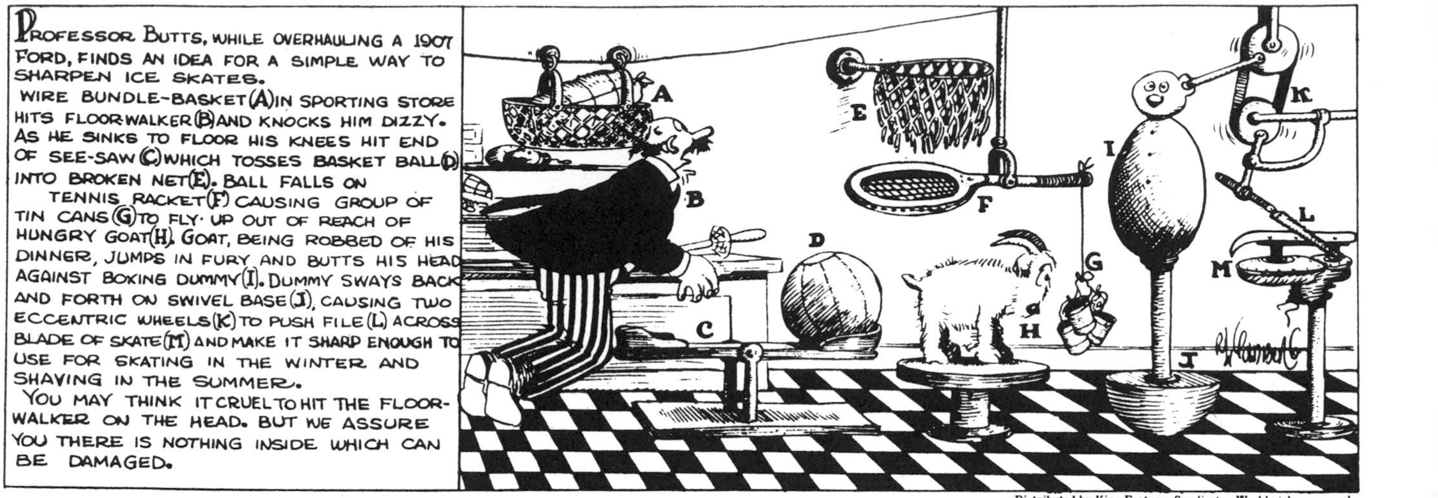
PROFESSOR BUTTS, WHILE OVERHAULING A 1907 FORD, FINDS AN IDEA FOR A SIMPLE WAY TO SHARPEN ICE SKATES.
WIRE BUNDLE-BASKET (A) IN SPORTING STORE HITS FLOORWALKER (B) AND KNOCKS HIM DIZZY. AS HE SINKS TO FLOOR HIS KNEES HIT END OF SEE-SAW (C) WHICH TOSSES BASKET BALL (D) INTO BROKEN NET (E). BALL FALLS ON TENNIS RACKET (F) CAUSING GROUP OF TIN CANS (G) TO FLY UP OUT OF REACH OF HUNGRY GOAT (H). GOAT, BEING ROBBED OF HIS DINNER, JUMPS IN FURY AND BUTTS HIS HEAD AGAINST BOXING DUMMY (I). DUMMY SWAYS BACK AND FORTH ON SWIVEL BASE (J), CAUSING TWO ECCENTRIC WHEELS (K) TO PUSH FILE (L) ACROSS BLADE OF SKATE (M) AND MAKE IT SHARP ENOUGH TO USE FOR SKATING IN THE WINTER AND SHAVING IN THE SUMMER.
YOU MAY THINK IT CRUEL TO HIT THE FLOOR-WALKER ON THE HEAD. BUT WE ASSURE YOU THERE IS NOTHING INSIDE WHICH CAN BE DAMAGED.
A
B
C
D
E
F
G
H
I
J
K
L
M

Rube Goldberg is one of the old-time cartoonists who developed a special kind of silly humor. The cartoon shown here is typical of the kind of feather-brained invention that he is famous for.

historians believe that the comics — like jazz music — are one of the major contributions that America has made to 20th-century culture.

Some cartoons and comic strip characters reproduced in this book are, unfortunately, no longer being drawn. But they are so wild and funny and imaginative that they are worth looking at. They are important because they are part of the history of comics. Comics, though, are a temporary art form. Newspapers turn yellow and crumple. Magazines get thrown away or are forgotten in dusty attics or dark closets. Even the funniest events or the most exciting adventures are soon forgotten. And many cartoon characters exist only as long as the cartoonist exists. Unhappily, when he dies or retires, the comic strip may go along with him.

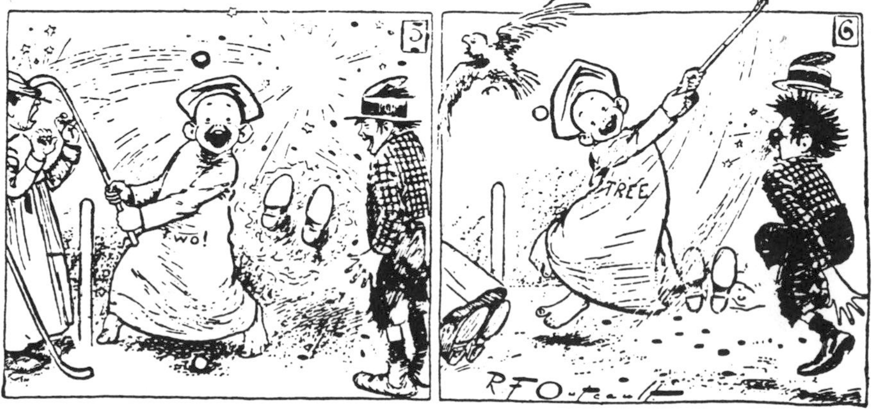
5
WO!
6
TREE

One of the first characters to appear in American comics was this strange-looking fellow by R. F. Outcault. He was called the "Yellow Kid" and managed constantly to get himself into the wildest predicaments.

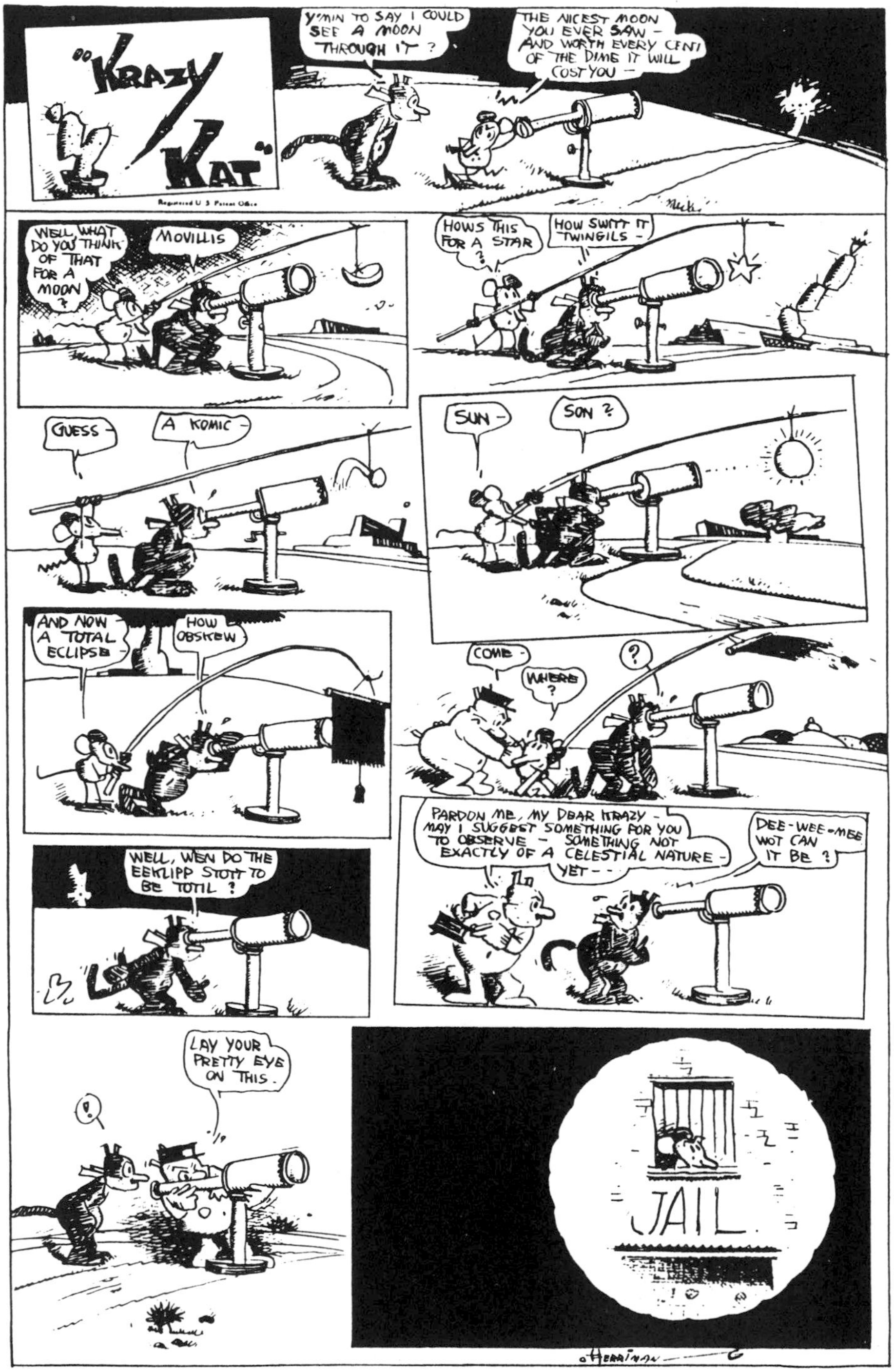
"Krazy Kat"
Y'MIN TO SAY I COULD SEE A MOON THROUGH IT ?
THE NICEST MOON YOU EVER SAW - AND WORTH EVERY CENT OF THE DIME IT WILL COST YOU -
WELL, WHAT DO YOU THINK OF THAT FOR A MOON ?
MOVILLIS
HOWS THIS FOR A STAR ?
HOW SWITT IT TWINGILS -
GUESS -
A KOMIC -
SUN -
SON ?
AND NOW A TOTAL ECLIPSE -
HOW OBSKEW
COME -
WHERE ?
?
WELL, WEN DO THE EEKLIPP STOTT TO BE TOTIL ?
PARDON ME, MY DEAR KRAZY - MAY I SUGGEST SOMETHING FOR YOU TO OBSERVE - SOMETHING NOT EXACTLY OF A CELESTIAL NATURE - YET - -
DEE-WEE-MEE WOT CAN IT BE ?
LAY YOUR PRETTY EYE ON THIS.
!
JAIL
Herriman

George Herriman's *Krazy Kat* is an old, unusual, and quite crazy comic strip that many people think is the best thing that ever appeared. The attraction is the offbeat, poetic humor, the strange settings, peculiar cast of characters, and the completely messed-up language used. *Krazy Kat* hasn't been published in a great many years, but there is still such a large and enthusiastic following that the old episodes are often reprinted.

FIRE!
1-18
© 1982 King Features Syndicate, Inc. World rights reserved.
MOOB!
YOU PUT THE SHELL IN BACKWARDS!!
MORT WALKER

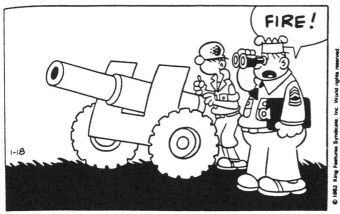

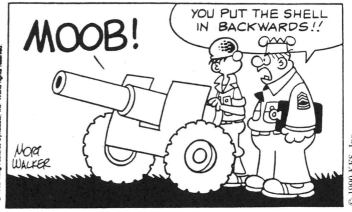

This comic strip consists of two panels. It is from *Beetle Bailey,* which is written and drawn by Mort Walker.

THE COMIC STRIP

The most common kind of cartoon is the comic strip. It is usually three or four pictures and text, lined up in a row. It is a *strip* of pictures. In most newspapers the comic strips are gathered together on one page. There may be six or more strips on a page, as well as some one-picture cartoons and perhaps a puzzle or two.

Some comic strips are comical, with the last picture or "panel" delivering the punch line. (The framed box in which picture and text appear is called a "panel.") There are other comic strips that are not the least bit funny. They tell a story that continues from one day to the next. In the case of the full-color Sunday papers, a comic strip usually has more room and can spread out somewhat. It will sometimes take up as much as half a page.

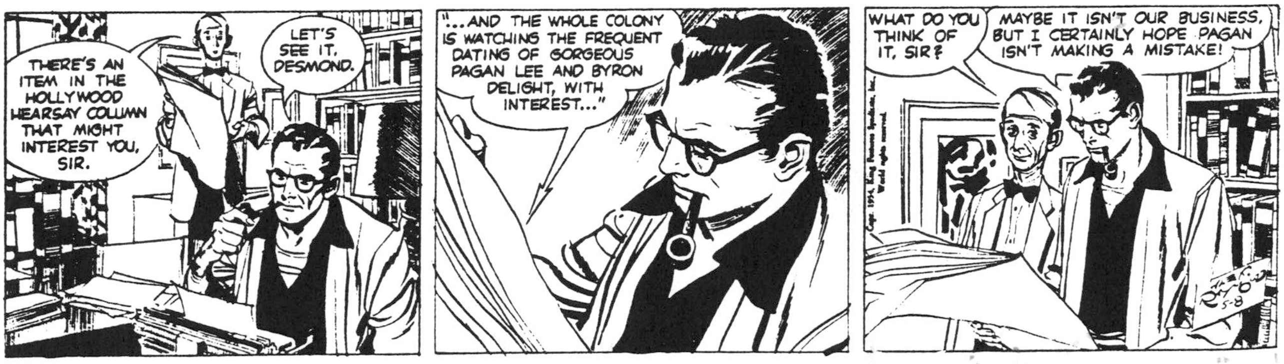
THERE'S AN ITEM IN THE HOLLYWOOD HEARSAY COLUMN THAT MIGHT INTEREST YOU, SIR.
LET'S SEE IT, DESMOND.
"...AND THE WHOLE COLONY IS WATCHING THE FREQUENT DATING OF GORGEOUS PAGAN LEE AND BYRON DELIGHT, WITH INTEREST..."
WHAT DO YOU THINK OF IT, SIR?
MAYBE IT ISN'T OUR BUSINESS, BUT I CERTAINLY HOPE PAGAN ISN'T MAKING A MISTAKE!

This sequence from *Rip Kirby* is by Alex Raymond. It is part of a long, dramatic story.▲

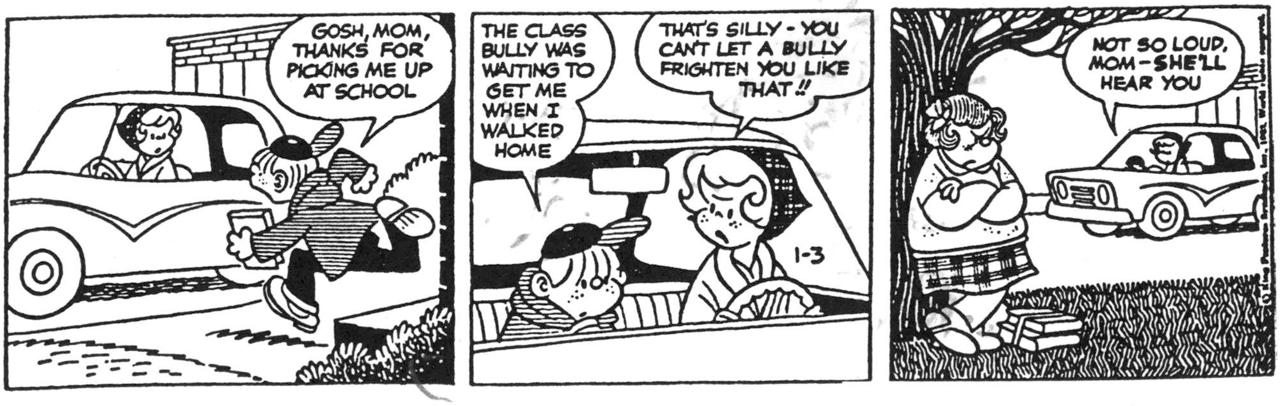
GOSH, MOM, THANKS FOR PICKING ME UP AT SCHOOL
THE CLASS BULLY WAS WAITING TO GET ME WHEN I WALKED HOME
THAT'S SILLY - YOU CAN'T LET A BULLY FRIGHTEN YOU LIKE THAT!!
1-3
NOT SO LOUD, MOM - SHE'LL HEAR YOU

The three-panel strip here is from *Hi and Lois* and is a "partnership" affair — the writing by Mort Walker and the drawing by Dik Browne.▲

In this one, long strip Redeye and friend are wondering why the fish aren't biting. This comic strip is produced by Bill Yates and Mel Casson.▼

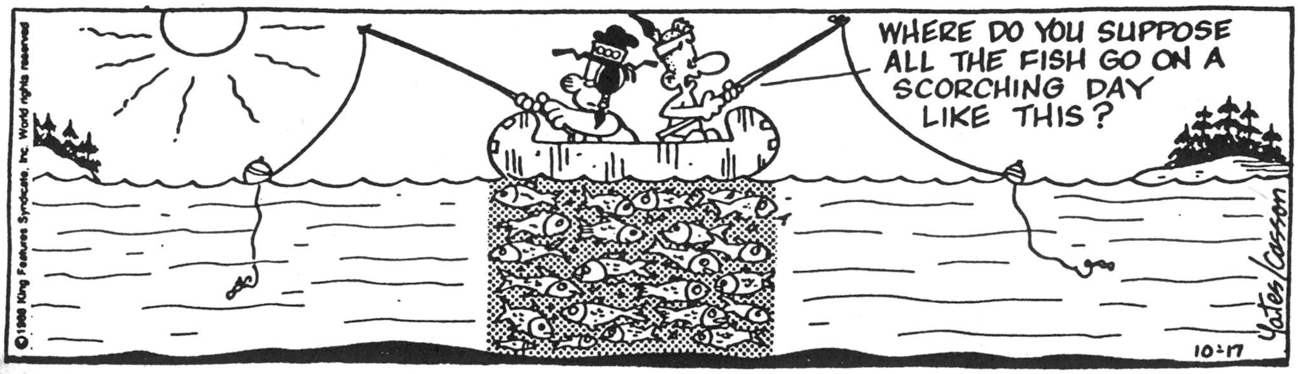
WHERE DO YOU SUPPOSE ALL THE FISH GO ON A SCORCHING DAY LIKE THIS?
Yates/Casson
10-17

In most cases the drawing shows what is happening. But to fully understand what is going on you must often read the dialogue. This combination of picture and written word is what is so special about comic strips, and cartoons in general — and what makes them so different from all other forms of communication.

Characters from cartoon strips have become part of the world's language and culture. They have achieved international fame. Some scholars have claimed that the cartoon strip is the world's most popular art form. Nearly everybody knows who Superman is. How about Dick Tracy, Orphan Annie, Good Old Charlie Brown, Beetle Bailey, Hägar the Horrible, Mickey Mouse, and Popeye?

Sometimes a comic strip will be rather elaborate, like this episode from *Sam and Silo* by Dumas. It is actually a mini-story with a lot going on in just a small amount of space. Seven panels of various sizes and shapes are used here.

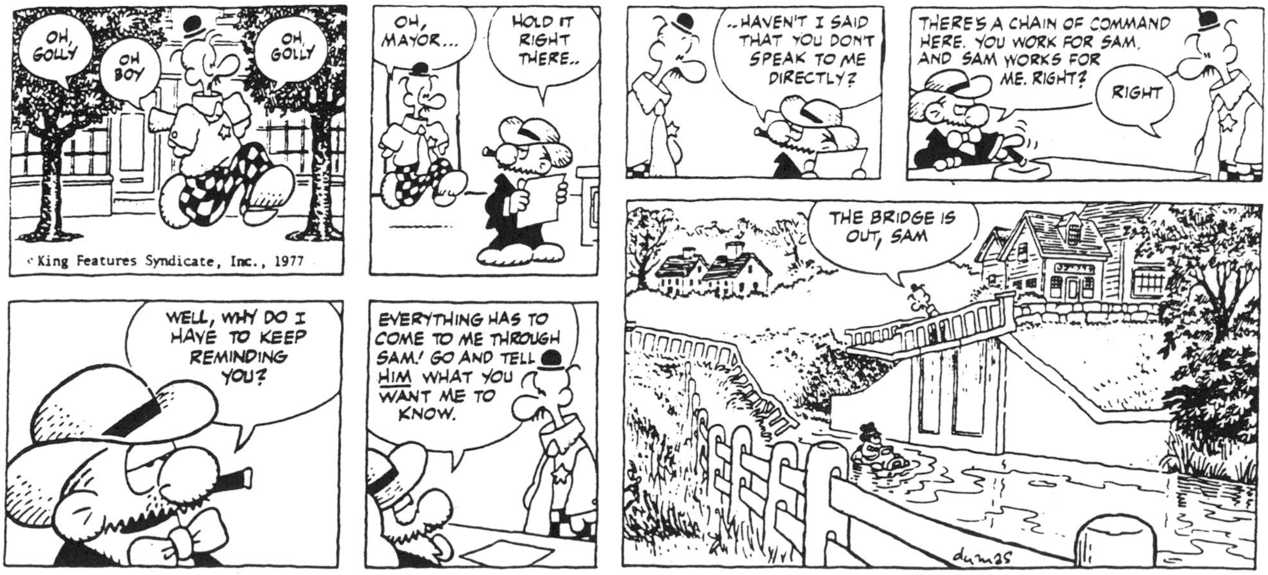
OH, GOLLY
OH BOY
OH, GOLLY
© King Features Syndicate, Inc., 1977
OH, MAYOR...
HOLD IT RIGHT THERE..
..HAVEN'T I SAID THAT YOU DON'T SPEAK TO ME DIRECTLY?
THERE'S A CHAIN OF COMMAND HERE. YOU WORK FOR SAM, AND SAM WORKS FOR ME. RIGHT?
RIGHT
WELL, WHY DO I HAVE TO KEEP REMINDING YOU?
EVERYTHING HAS TO COME TO ME THROUGH SAM! GO AND TELL HIM WHAT YOU WANT ME TO KNOW.
THE BRIDGE IS OUT, SAM
dumas

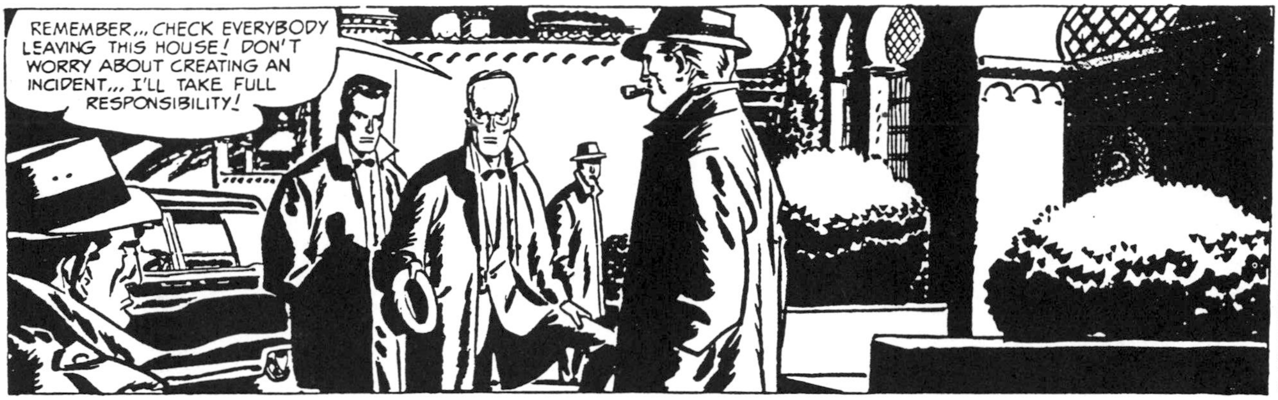
REMEMBER... CHECK EVERYBODY LEAVING THIS HOUSE! DON'T WORRY ABOUT CREATING AN INCIDENT... I'LL TAKE FULL RESPONSIBILITY!

In some cases, an elongated panel like this will best describe an action. In this scene there are many characters and the mood is set by the rather complicated background. Several small panels would not be able to make so dramatic a scene. This episode is from *Johnny Hazard* by Frank Robbins.▲

Not all of these characters may be familiar to you because they may not be in the newspapers that you see or they may no longer be produced. But most of them do still appear in the hundreds of newspapers that circulate here and abroad. Some cartoons appear in over two thousand papers. There are very few newspapers that carry no cartoons at all. Some characters have even been the basis for movies or TV programs or Broadway musical shows.

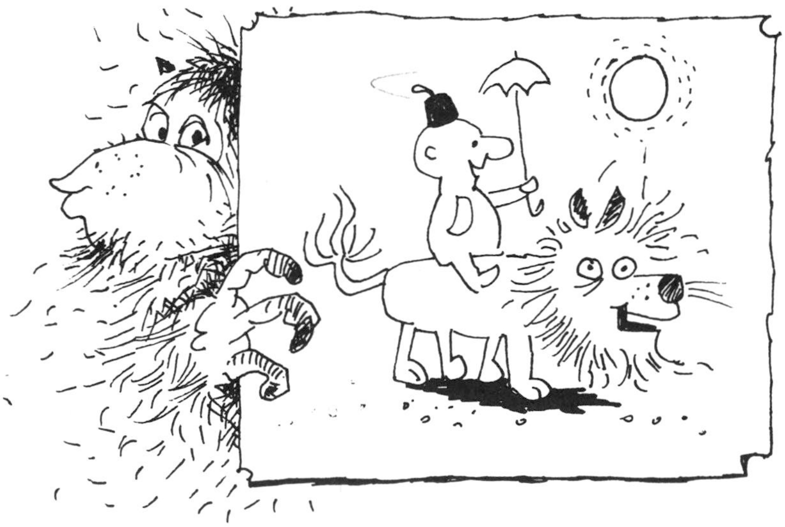

From time to time some very odd creatures will appear in comic strips.

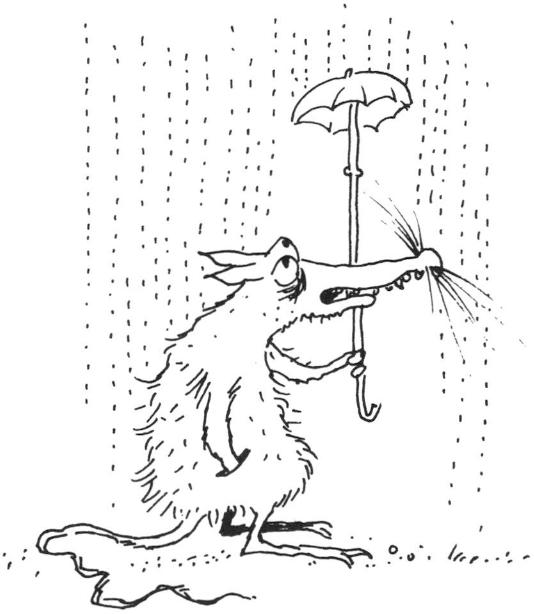

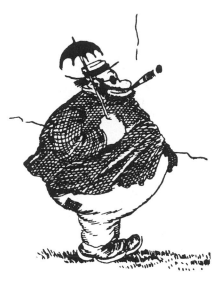

BEING FUNNY

There are many different kinds of humor. And not everyone agrees on what is funny. What is hilarious to one person may not get even a smile from somebody else. But there are some things that are sure to amuse even the grimmest old grouch. Who, for example, wouldn't laugh at the cartoons on these pages?

Certain things that cartoonists deal with are just naturally funny. They are events that are unexpected, illogical, or greatly exaggerated. The basis for many jokes lies in actions that are surprising or that have to do with misunderstandings and confusion.

I'D LIKE A BLUEBERRY...
...PIE
ZOPPO
I HATE THESE FAST-FOOD PLACES
7-29
DIK BROWNE

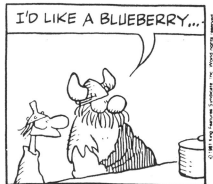

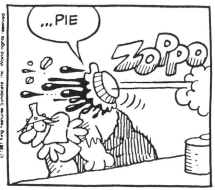

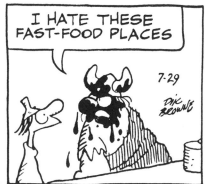

In some comic strips, like this one by Dik Browne, drawing and writing go very much hand in hand. Both are essential. If the strip didn't show the pie flying in the face of Hägar the Horrible at the same time he was saying he didn't like fast food places, there would be no gag at all. This combination of picture and written word is what makes cartoons so special.

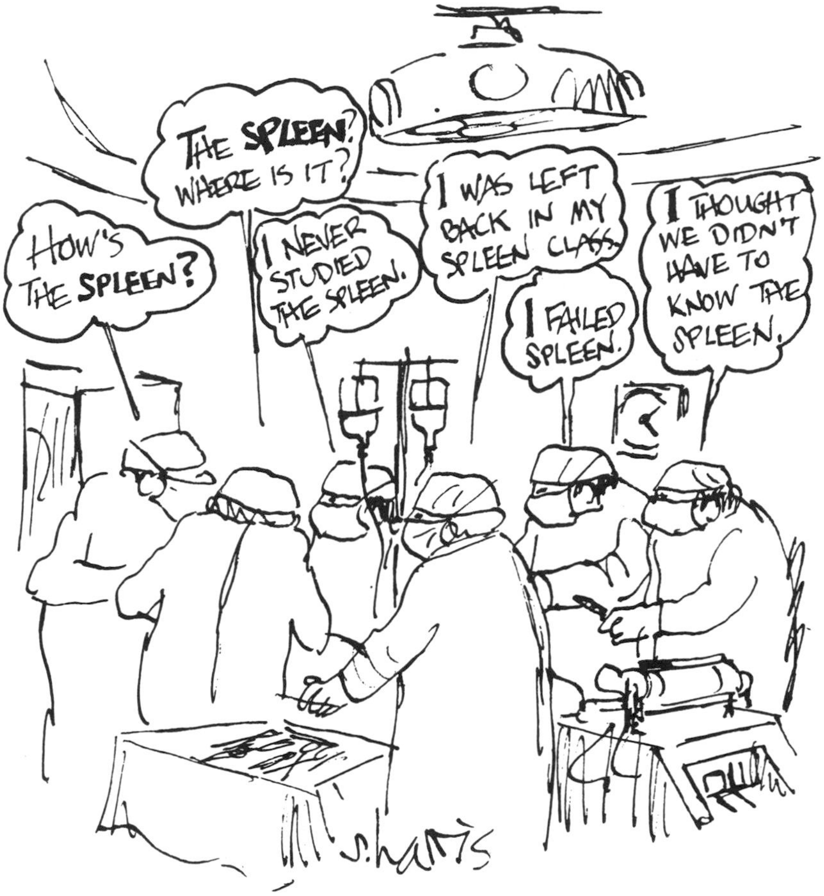
HOW'S THE SPLEEN?
THE SPLEEN? WHERE IS IT?
I NEVER STUDIED THE SPLEEN.
I WAS LEFT BACK IN MY SPLEEN CLASS.
I FAILED SPLEEN.
I THOUGHT WE DIDN'T HAVE TO KNOW THE SPLEEN.
S. HARRIS

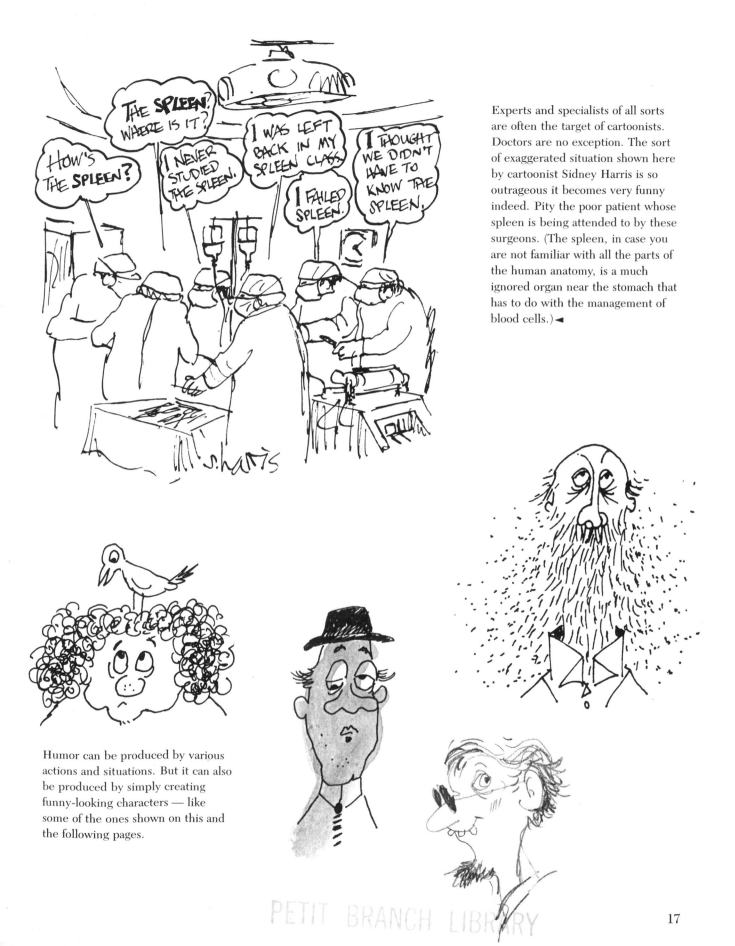

Experts and specialists of all sorts are often the target of cartoonists. Doctors are no exception. The sort of exaggerated situation shown here by cartoonist Sidney Harris is so outrageous it becomes very funny indeed. Pity the poor patient whose spleen is being attended to by these surgeons. (The spleen, in case you are not familiar with all the parts of the human anatomy, is a much ignored organ near the stomach that has to do with the management of blood cells.) ◄

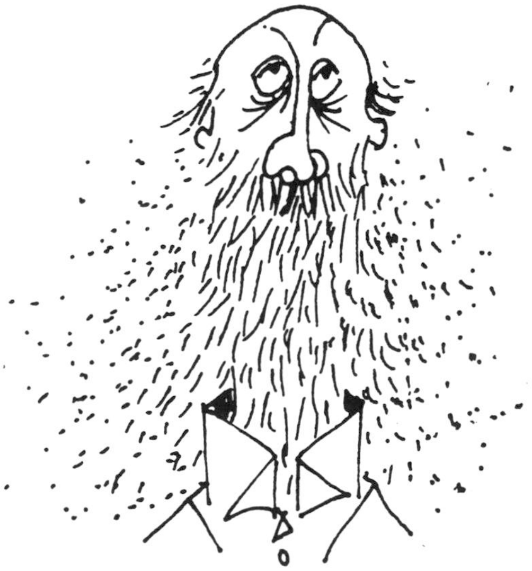

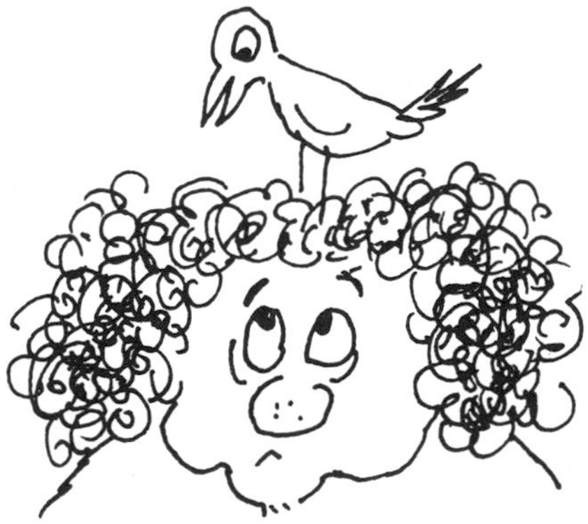

Humor can be produced by various actions and situations. But it can also be produced by simply creating funny-looking characters — like some of the ones shown on this and the following pages.

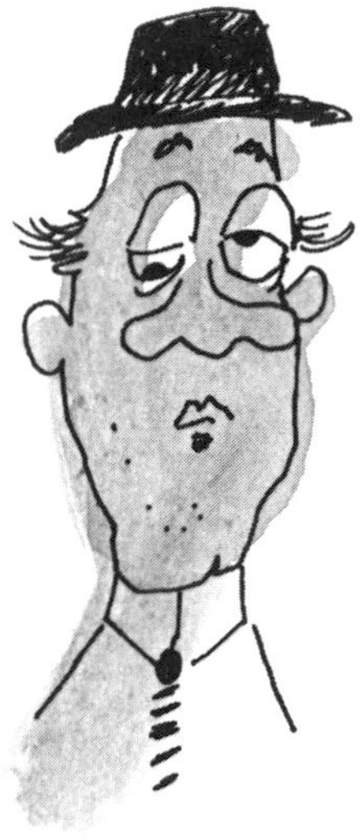

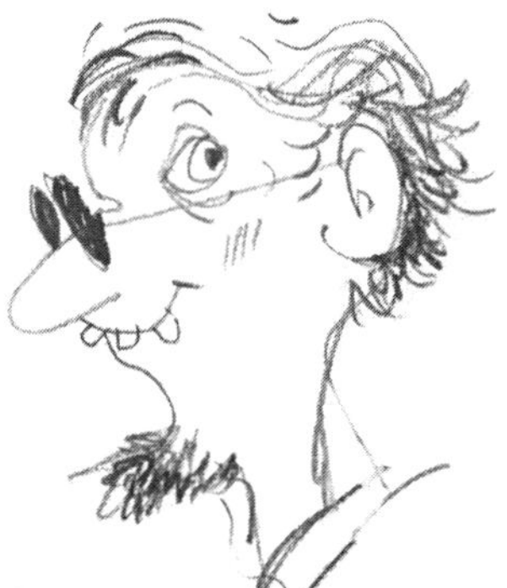

The cartoonist calls his funny stories "gags." The one-picture cartoon is called a "gag panel." Cartoonists who produce comic material work hard at getting their gags. Even the cartoonist with the best sense of humor has to be constantly on the lookout for funny situations and amusing goings-on that can be used in his comic strip or cartoon.

Some of the best cartoons are based not only on funny events but on funny characters. Strange and unusual characters are

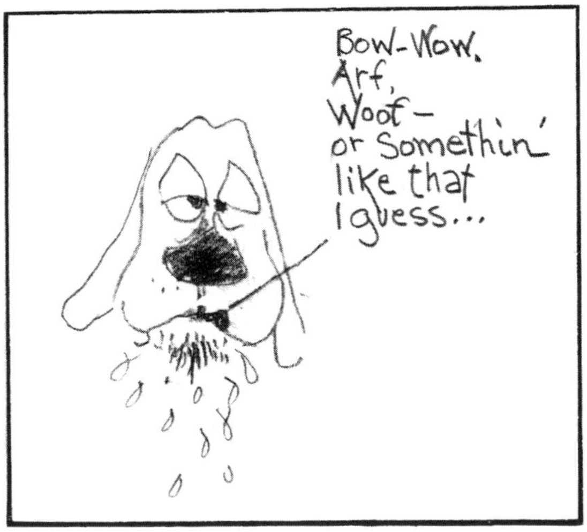
Bow-Wow. Arf, Woof – or Somethin' like that I guess...

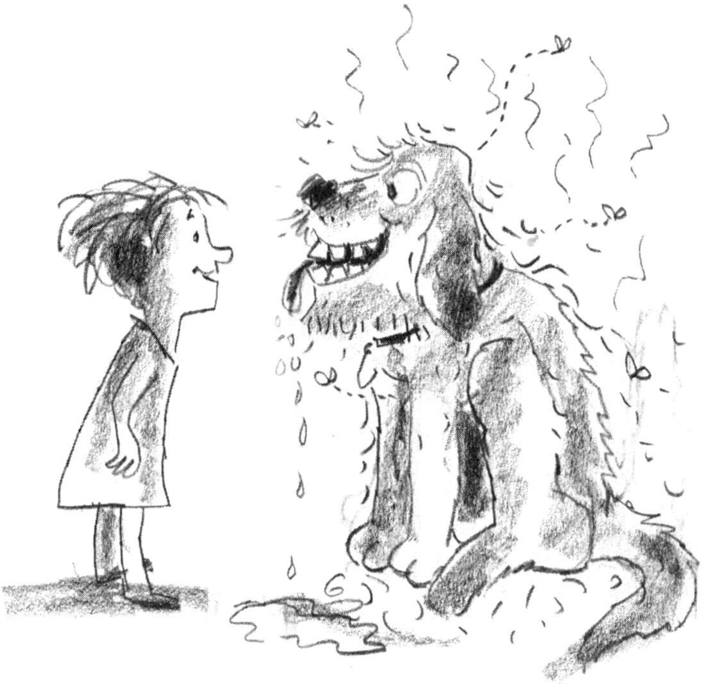

"OH MY, WHAT A CUTE, LITTLE, BEAUTIFUL DOGGIE!"

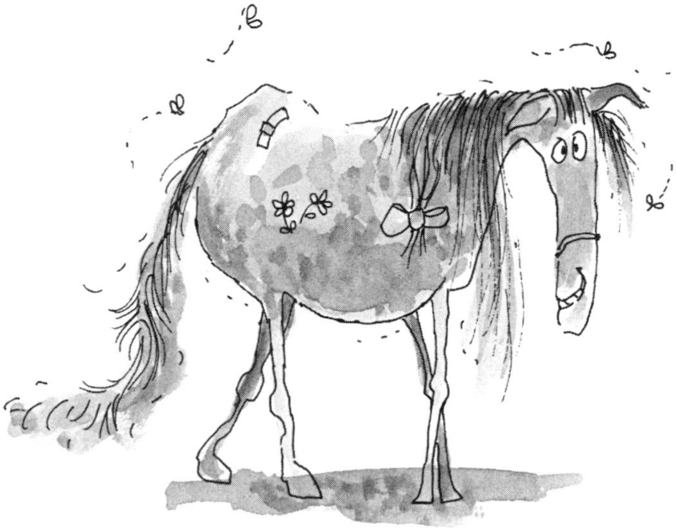

Animals lend themselves to the cartoonist's sense of humor. Ordinary four-legged creatures — cats, dogs, horses — as well as more fancy types, are usually funny when exaggerated, shown in human situations, or when engaged in conversation.

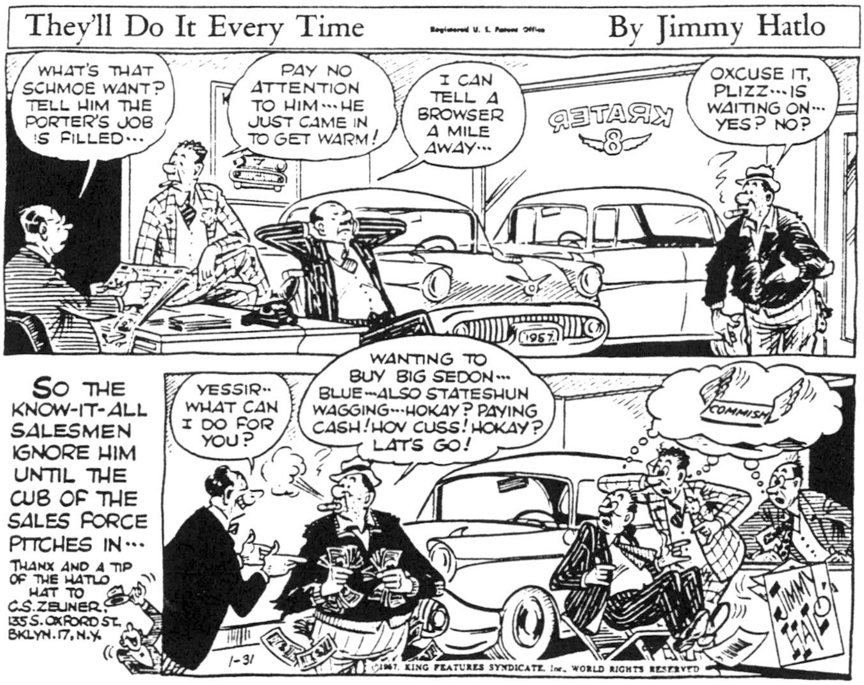
They'll Do It Every Time
By Jimmy Hatlo
WHAT'S THAT SCHMOE WANT? TELL HIM THE PORTER'S JOB IS FILLED···
PAY NO ATTENTION TO HIM···HE JUST CAME IN TO GET WARM!
I CAN TELL A BROWSER A MILE AWAY···
KRATER 8
OXCUSE IT, PLIZZ···IS WAITING ON··· YES? NO?
1957
SO THE KNOW-IT-ALL SALESMEN IGNORE HIM UNTIL THE CUB OF THE SALES FORCE PITCHES IN···
THANX AND A TIP OF THE HATLO HAT TO C.S. ZEUNER, 135 S. OXFORD ST. BKLYN. 17, N.Y.
YESSIR·· WHAT CAN I DO FOR YOU?
WANTING TO BUY BIG SEDON··· BLUE··ALSO STATESHUN WAGGING···HOKAY? PAYING CASH! HOV CUSS! HOKAY? LAT'S GO!
COMMISH
JIMMY HATLO
1-31
KING FEATURES SYNDICATE, Inc., WORLD RIGHTS RESERVED

They'll Do It Every Time by Jimmy Hatlo is a very popular cartoon that has a gentle kind of satire of human nature. It has been running in many newspapers for a very long time.

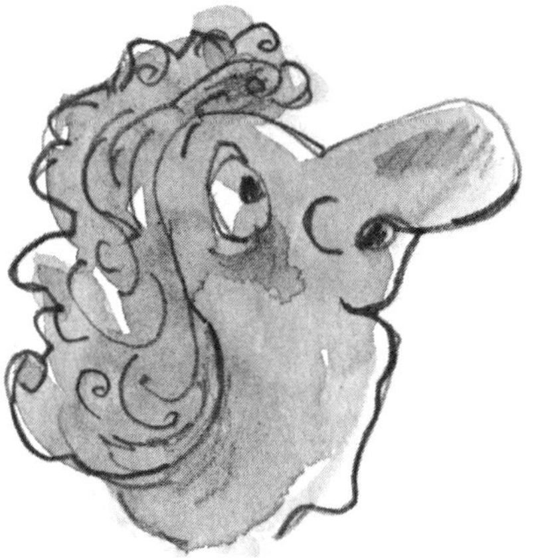

A great many cartoonists seem to enjoy drawing faces with large noses. As a matter of fact, most cartoon characters, except for the realistic ones, have large noses. Sometimes huge! In this cartoon the nose is put to some practical use.▼

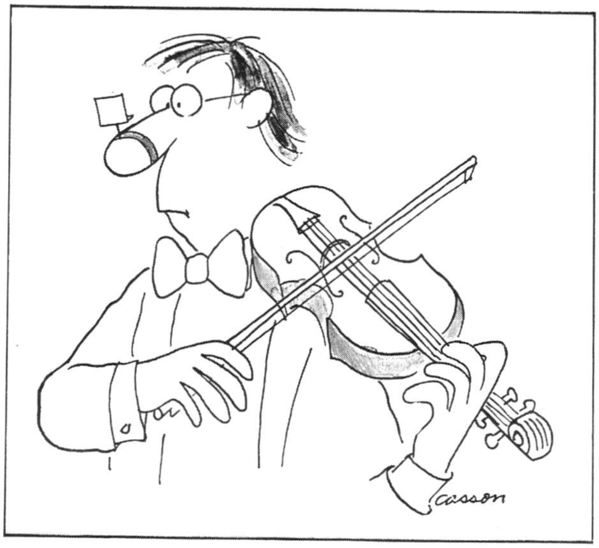
casson

"YOU WANTED TO KNOW WHAT TO DO WITH WATERMELON SEEDS?"

Mothers-in-law take an awful lot of abuse from cartoonists, and that is certainly the case with this *Bringing Up Father* strip by Frank Johnson.▼

MY MOTHER'S COMING TO VISIT!

WILL YOU CALL MY DOCTOR AND MAKE AN APPOINTMENT FOR ME

FRANK JOHNSON 6-20

© KFS 1986

ARE YOU ILL?

NOT NOW!

...BUT I WILL BE WHEN YOUR MOTHER ARRIVES!

© 1990 KFS, Inc.

This rather wild-looking chef is fun to look at, not because he is doing anything special, but simply because of his strange expression, peculiar clothing, and because of the style of drawing, which uses an unusual jagged but carefully drawn line.

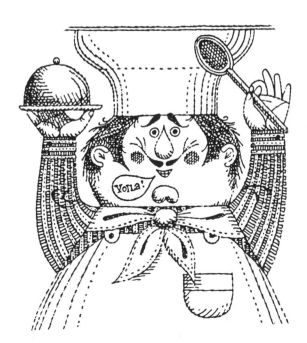

amusing even if they just stand there without doing anything. They just look funny because of their faces, their strange clothing, their peculiar gestures. Popeye is a strange-looking fellow. So are Beetle Bailey, Dennis the Menace, and Archie, not to mention a great variety of odd-looking dogs, cats, tigers, and other strange animals.

Some cartoons from many years ago, as well as a few from the present, are funny in a special way. They have a wild, imaginative kind of fantasy. Anything could happen in these cartoons — and usually did. Submarines surfaced in bathtubs. Trolley cars bounced along in the most unreal way. A mouse could throw a brick at a cat while having a conversation with a bull-dog policeman. And an alligator could smoke a cigar while discussing current events with a possum. Where else but in the comics could you find such strange and wonderful happenings?

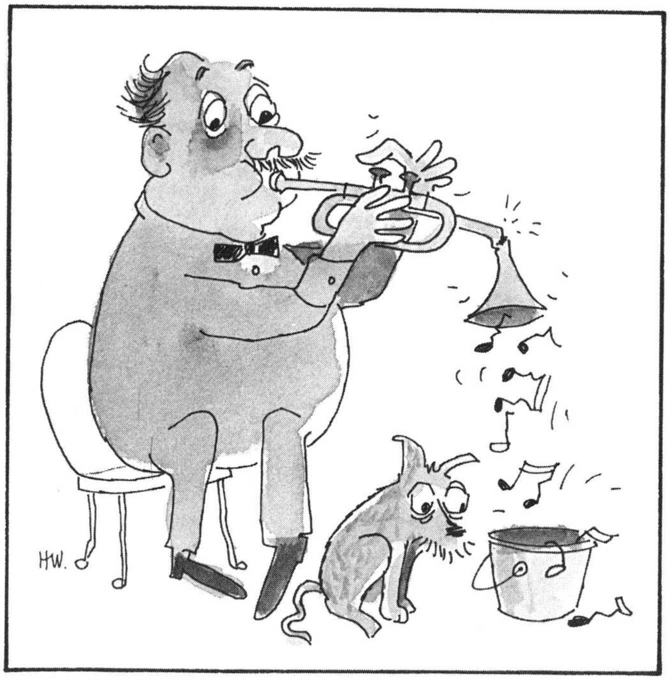
H.W.

Nonsense makes good sense in cartoons. The most impossible and silly situation makes the funniest cartoon. Who ever heard of a trumpet breaking and ragged notes falling out into a bucket while a puzzled dog sits there watching?

THE GAG PANEL

In a comic strip there are several panels where a situation can be built up leading to a final punch line or funny ending. It is like a very short, amusing story. On the other hand, the one-picture cartoon, or "gag" panel, as it is called by cartoonists, has to tell its story in just one picture. It often has a caption underneath. The humor must all be there in the single picture and caption.

Because this kind of cartoon has to tell its story all at once, a faster and more immediate kind of humor is used. As you can see from the cartoons shown here, the gag is understandable right away. No conversation or complicated events appear beforehand.

The artists who do this kind of cartoon develop their own brand of humor as well as their own drawing style. Charles Addams was known for the creepy-crawly characters and settings that he always used. And other cartoonists can be identified right away by their way of drawing as well as by the kind of humor they are partial to.

The gag panel is found in newspapers where there isn't room for something larger, and as a change from the strip cartoon. But it is found most often in magazines. The very early cartoons that appeared in the 1800s in English magazines were mostly gag panels — though nobody at that time thought to call them that.

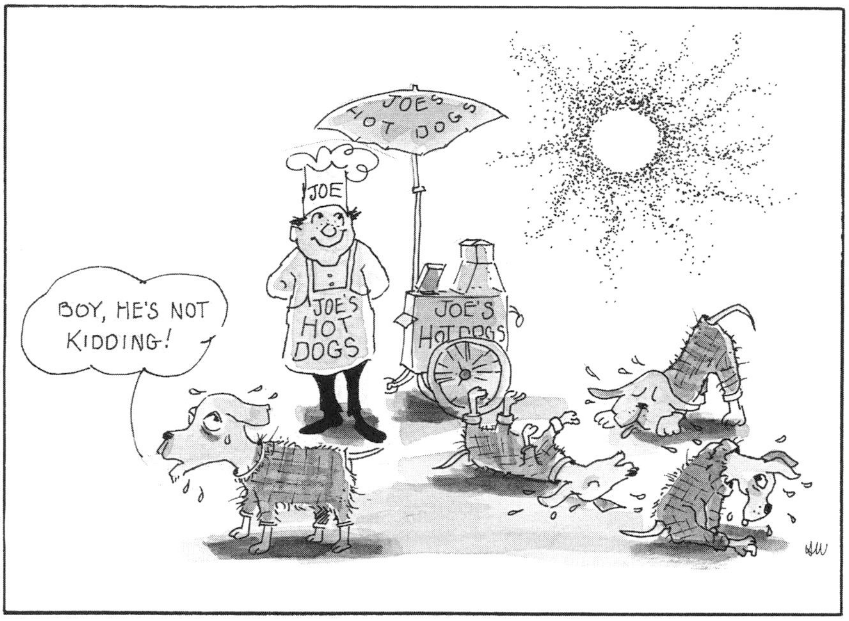
JOE'S HOT DOGS
JOE
JOE'S HOT DOGS
JOE'S HOT DOGS
BOY, HE'S NOT KIDDING!

In this gag panel the dogs are shown overdressed and uncomfortably hot while the not-too-intelligent-looking hot dog man is standing by his wagon daydreaming or thinking about selling his hot dogs. Everything is in the one picture.

A gag panel often has a caption under the picture. But in this case there is no caption. One of the "hot dogs," looking very uncomfortable indeed, is delivering the punch line!

With a gag panel the drawing is particularly important. With only one panel to work with there is no time or space for a lot of preliminary action that can build up to the punch line. The drawing has to show the characters and the setting and just what the action is. In many cases the gag panel will use no words at all. It is often possible for the drawing by itself to tell the whole story.

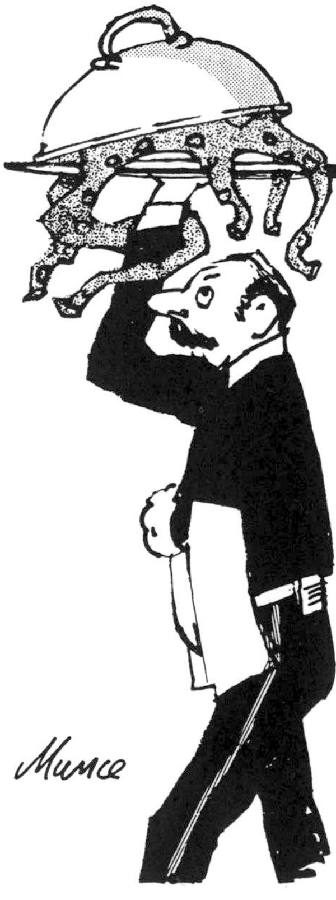

The cartoonist, looking for something funny, will often take a very ordinary, unfunny event, and add something strange or unexpected to it. A waiter carrying a tray isn't very funny. But put a live octopus on the tray and a weird and funny situation is created. Notice the expression on the waiter's face as the octopus is about to wrap a tentacle around his wrist!

Another kind of funny situation develops when an unreal situation is treated in a realistic way. Who ever heard of a dog driving a car? So it is rather startling when a very serious state trooper very seriously questions the poor dog who probably ran through a stop sign or a red light . . . and no doubt, left his driver's license at home! We may ask who is unreal here, the dog, the trooper, or maybe the cartoonist!

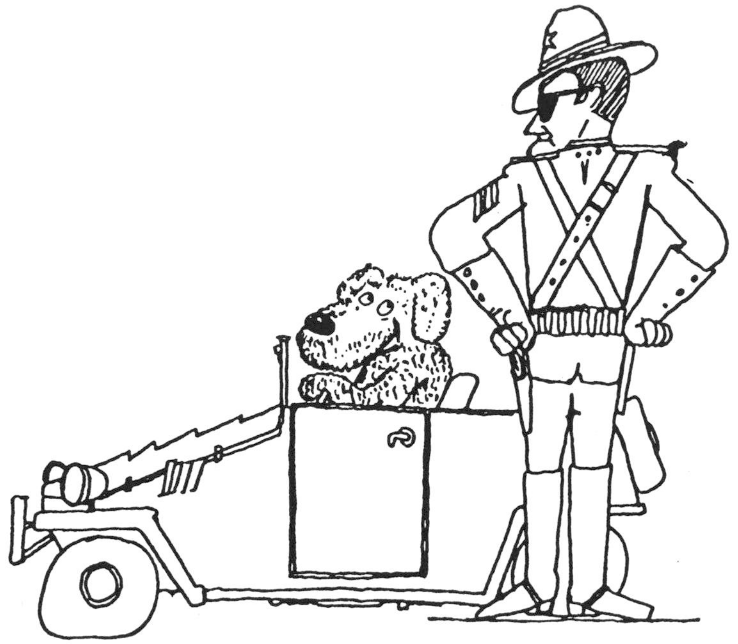

"... and I suppose you're going to tell me you forgot your driver's license!"

Sometimes a simple little joke can be built up into a major production by the piling on of a lot of silly or amusing detail — like the mangy cats and dogs, and the broken-down setting of the boat yard with the rather sad-looking boat.

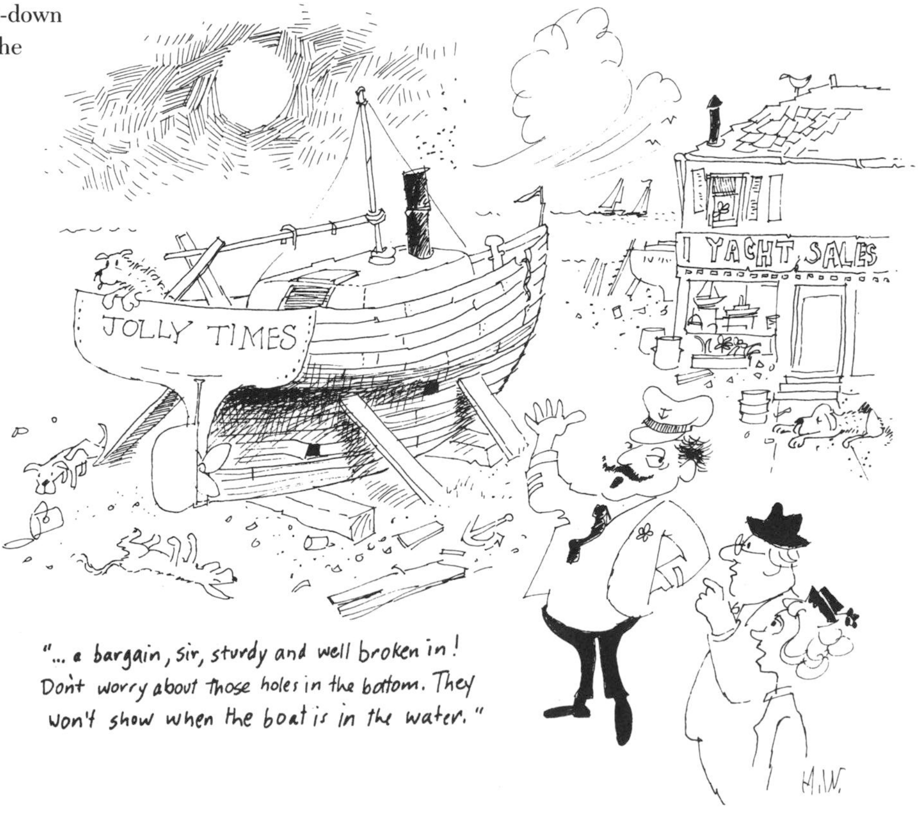
JOLLY TIMES
YACHT SALES
H.W.

"... a bargain, sir, sturdy and well broken in! Don't worry about those holes in the bottom. They won't show when the boat is in the water."

The cartoon below was first published over 150 years ago. It is by a famous English artist, George Cruikshank. At that time nobody would have thought to call it a "gag panel," though that is what it is. The very thin and frail-looking horses are, with good reason, getting rather upset as they look at the enormous passengers about to climb aboard the stagecoach they will have to pull. The horse who is saying, "Where is our friend Martin?" is referring to a member of Parliament by the name of Richard Martin who, in 1822, worked for the first laws that outlawed cruelty to animals.

One may wonder where those last three passengers are going to fit. Pity those poor horses! This is a typical cartoon situation where the humor comes from the gross exaggeration of the situation.

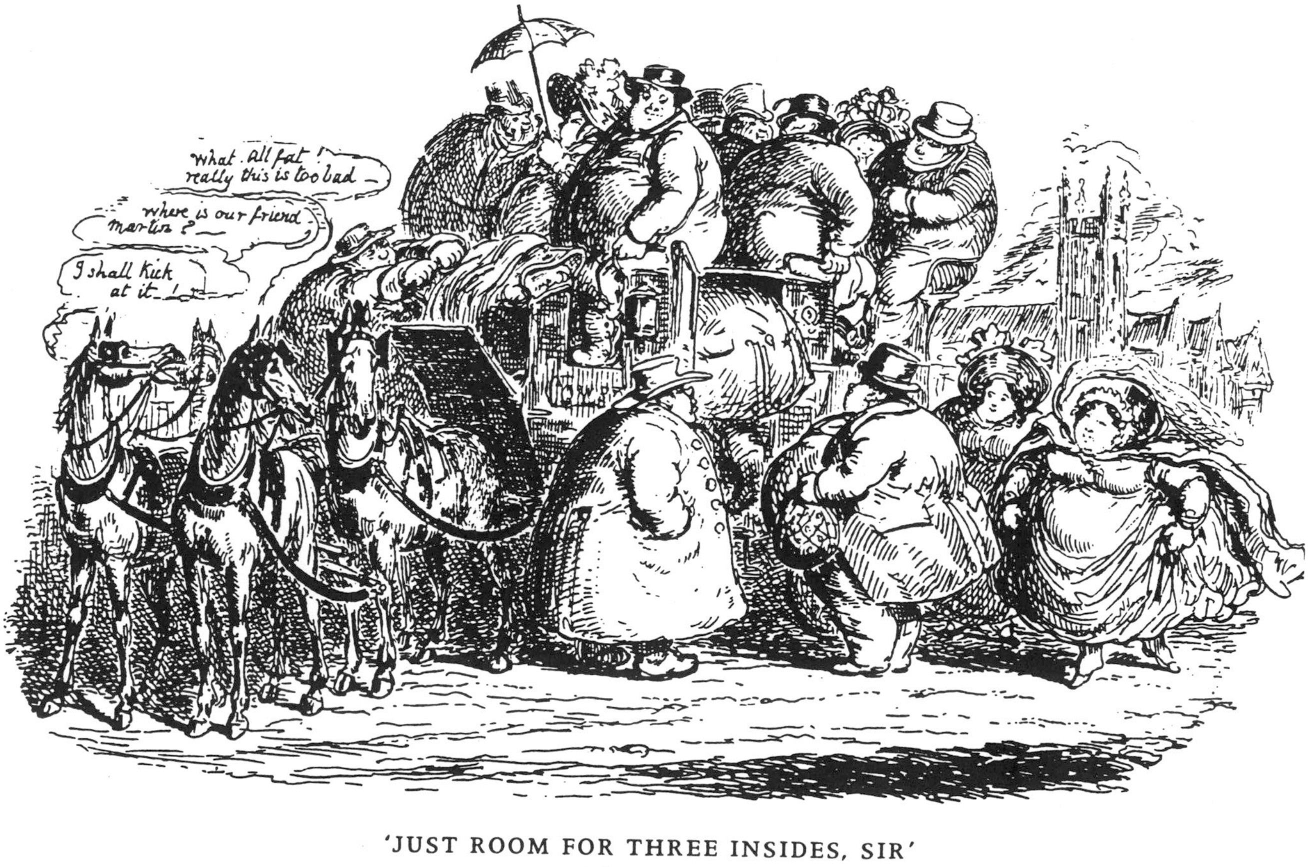
What. All fat! really this is too bad –
where is our friend Martin? –
I shall Kick at it–!

'JUST ROOM FOR THREE INSIDES, SIR'
February 1831

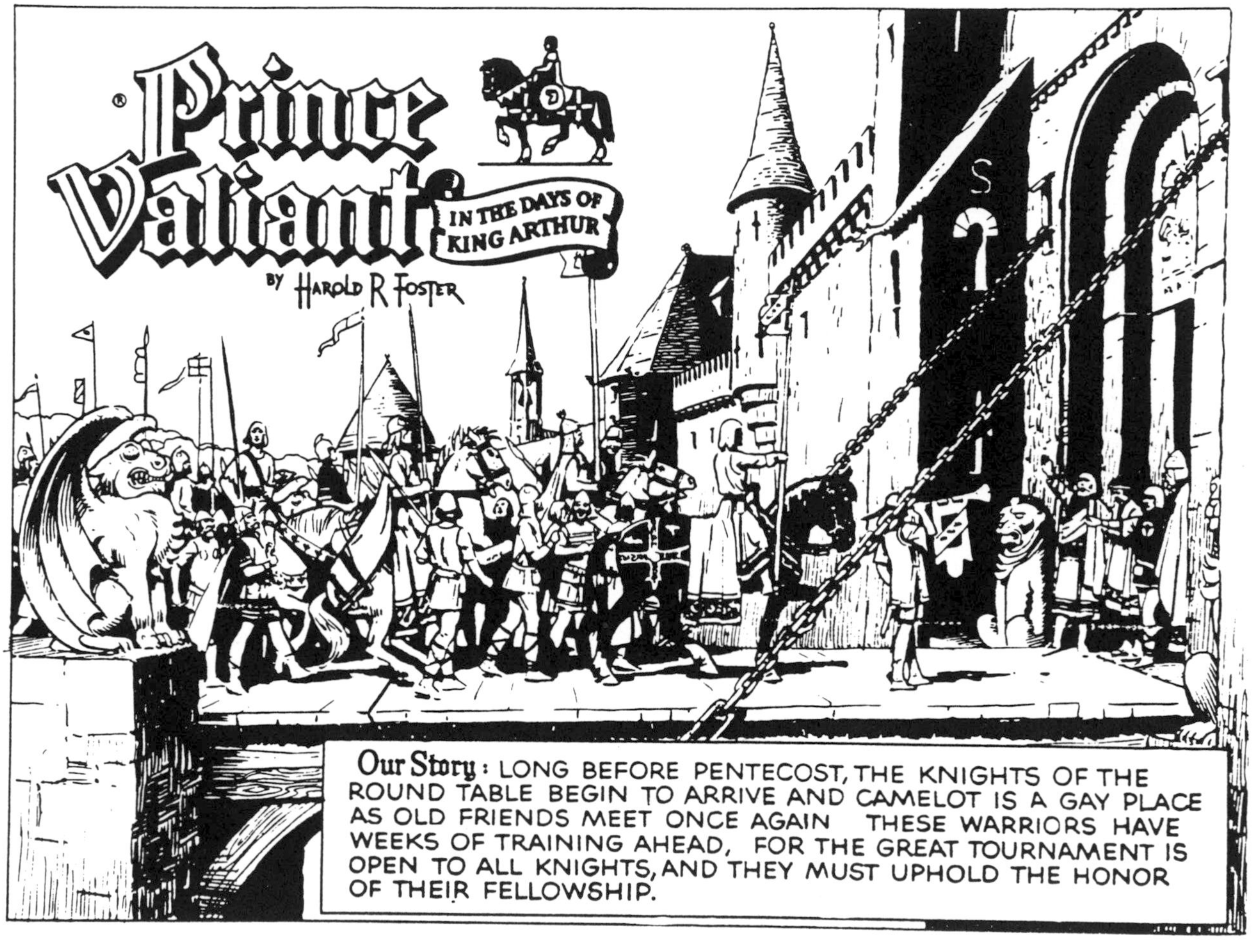
Prince Valiant
IN THE DAYS OF KING ARTHUR
BY HAROLD R FOSTER
Our Story: LONG BEFORE PENTECOST, THE KNIGHTS OF THE ROUND TABLE BEGIN TO ARRIVE AND CAMELOT IS A GAY PLACE AS OLD FRIENDS MEET ONCE AGAIN THESE WARRIORS HAVE WEEKS OF TRAINING AHEAD, FOR THE GREAT TOURNAMENT IS OPEN TO ALL KNIGHTS, AND THEY MUST UPHOLD THE HONOR OF THEIR FELLOWSHIP.

THE CARTOON STORY

The cartoonist is a writer as well as an illustrator. It isn't enough just to draw pictures. If the comic strip is a humorous one the cartoonist has to invent a humorous situation. If the comic strip tells a story there must be suspense and excitement. The reader must be made to care about what is happening and how it will all come out.

One cartoon story character who has been appearing for over 60 years is Popeye. During that time all sorts of stories have been told — everything from finding hidden treasure to weird adventures with some very strange people. Some of these supporting characters include Popeye's girl friend Olive Oyl, the Jeep, and an assortment of thugs that Popeye enjoys beating up. One friend is J. Wellington Wimpy, who has an out-of-control passion for hamburgers. The episode shown on this page deals with Wimpy's uncontrollable "hamburger lust."

IS THAT WIMPY COMING UP THE STREET?
YEAH, THA'S HIM. COMIN' HERE I SUSPOSE
THE WORLD'S CHAMPION MOOCHER IS AT THE DOOR. SHALL I LET HIM IN, POPEYE?
OKAY, OLIVE, I SUSPOSE HE COME OVER TO TELL ME THAT HE'D MOW MY LAWN FOR ME IF I HAD A LAWN TO MOW
YES, INDEED, MY FRIEND – I WOULD GLADLY MOW YOUR LAWN FOR YOU IF YOU HAD A LAWN TO MOW – HMM – OLD PAL, COULD YOU LET ME HAVE THE PRICE OF A SHOE-SHINE? I'M FAMISHED
WHY DON'T YA TRY TO AMOUNT TO SUMPIN', WIMPY? THE TROUBLE IS, YA GOT NO INTESTIMAL FORTNITUDE – AN' NO WILL-POWER
NO WILL POWER?
YOU ARE ALL DAMP, MY GOOD MAN – I HAVE A STRONG WILL – AYE, THE WILL POWER OF A NAPOLEON
I SEZ YA AIN'T, YA BLASTED JELLYFISH!!
THE IDEA, MISS OYL – POPEYE SAYING THAT I HAVE NO WILL-POWER
I'D GIVE ANYTHING IF I COULD SHOW HIM UP!!
GOOD MORNIN', JEEP – I SUSPOSE YA STILL GOT YER ABILIKY TO FORETELL THE FUTURE?
JEEP! JEEP!
THANK YOU TOO MUCH FOR THIS HAMBURGER
WAIT – I YAM GONER TEST YER WILL-POWER – I TOOK THIS MONEY OUT OF ME SAFE AN' –
$ 20,000
IF YA'LL SET THERE AN' HOLD THAT HAMBURGER FOR TEN MINUTES WITHOUT TAKIN' A BITE I'LL GIVE YA THIS $20,000
THAT WILL BE EASY
$ 20,000
POPEYE, YOU'RE THE BIGGEST SAP ON EARTH! WHY, YOU MUST BE CRAZY
YOU KNOW HE WON'T TAKE A BITE OF THAT HAMBURGER. HE'LL GET YOUR $20,000
SNIFF SNIFF
AND YOU'LL REALLY GIVE HIM THE MONEY IF HE HOLDS OFF TEN MINUTES?
CERTINGLY
POPEYE, IF HE HOLDS OFF ONE MINUTE MORE. HE'LL WIN
TWENTY SECONDS MORE AND YOUR MONEY WILL BE GONE
I AIN'T WORRIED
GET THEE BEHIND ME SATAN!
NO! NO!
NO! NO! YES! NO! YES! NO! NO! NO!
YES
NO
! !
ARF! ARF!
SNAP
$ 20,000
8-15
I DIDN'T TAKE NO CHANCE. I AST THE JEEP IF HE COULD DO IT.
WHAT A FOOL I AM!
SEGAR

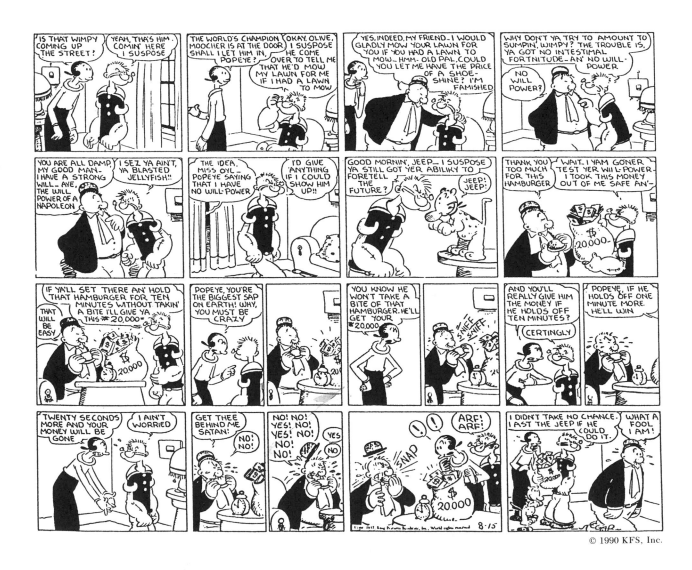

A story or dramatic cartoon strip is like a novel or short story. It must have all the good features of this kind of writing. It has one big advantage, though. It can use the drawings to explain and show quickly and in detail just what is going on. In this respect it is something like a TV soap opera or situation comedy. The comic strip has no need for a lot of written description. The picture tells all. The only writing needed is for the dialogue. Only comic strips can put writing and drawing so close together. It is this combination of picture and word that is so special.

In comic strips the characters are almost always talking. There is conversation — dialogue — going on all the time without a lot of written comment. This results in fast action with few distractions. There are, of course, exceptions. Sometimes it is necessary to explain complicated events. Some cartoons do have a lot of wordy conversation. And there are also cases where the action is shown in the drawings and there is no conversation at all.

A good deal of talk in a comic strip is in the form of dialect. Dialect is speech that differs from the ordinary because the person speaking comes from a not-ordinary background. For example, a cowboy might say, "Thunderation! They is still follerin' us!" An old sailor would have a different kind of speech. He might say, "Ahoy, ya lubbers!"

Since cartoons are filled with people who are talking and many

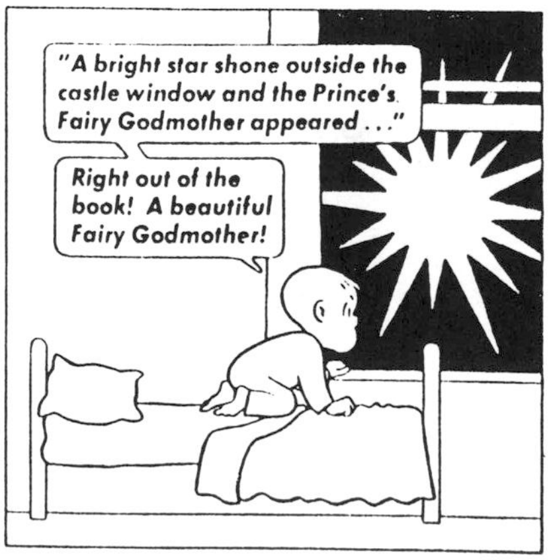
"A bright star shone outside the castle window and the Prince's Fairy Godmother appeared . . ."
Right out of the book! A beautiful Fairy Godmother!

Barnaby is a rather unusual cartoon story that, unfortunately, is no longer produced. It was written and drawn by Crockett Johnson, who has also done the well-known book *Harold and the Purple Crayon.* The brief sequence here shows Barnaby first meeting his fairy godfather, Mr. O'Malley, a rather paunchy little fellow with wings. He flies in a window, makes a bad landing, breaking his magic wand (his cigar), and then introduces himself.

Many famous old cartoons like *Barnaby* are still available, having been reprinted in book form.►

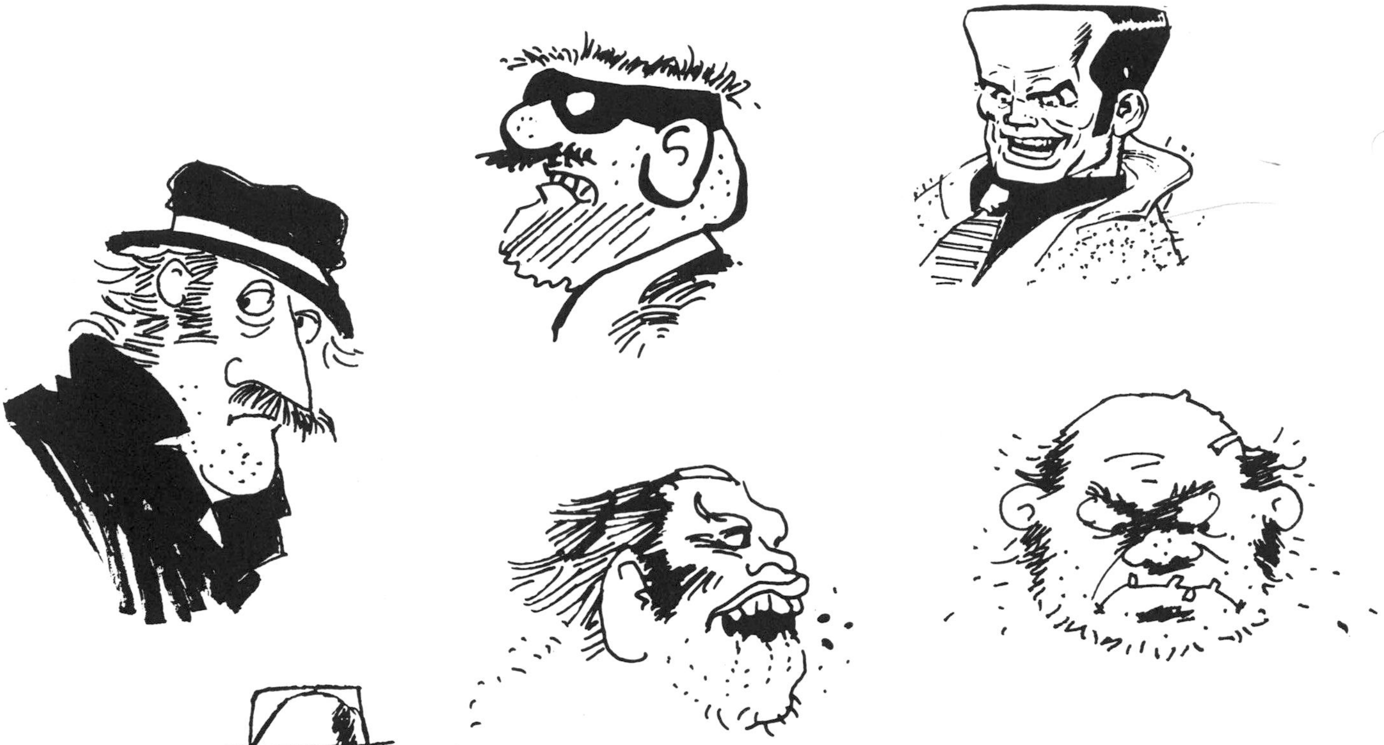

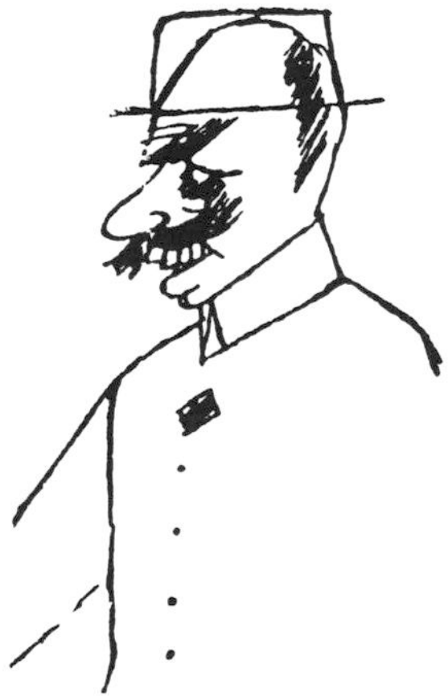

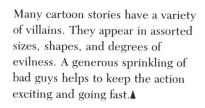

Many cartoon stories have a variety of villains. They appear in assorted sizes, shapes, and degrees of evilness. A generous sprinkling of bad guys helps to keep the action exciting and going fast.▲

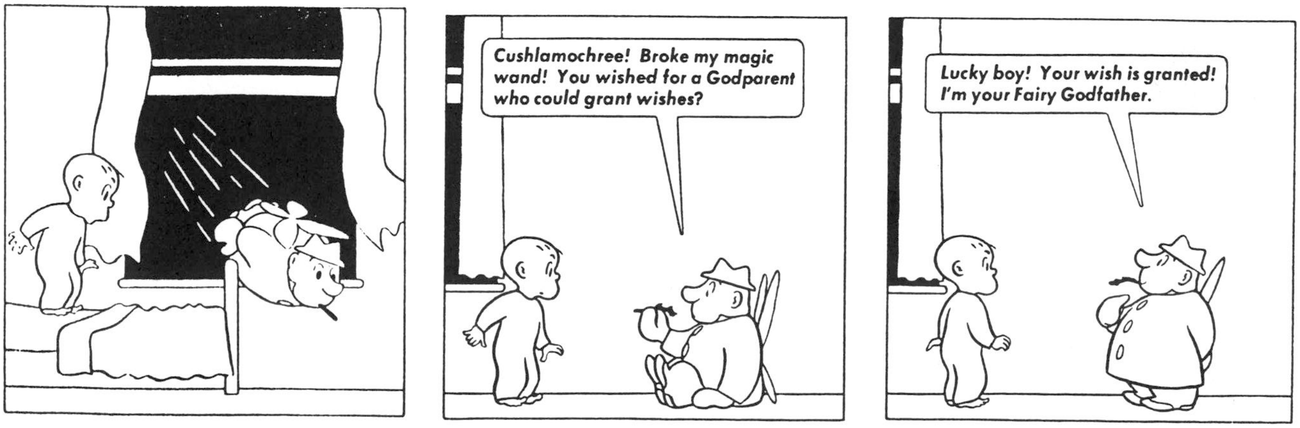

Cushlamochree! Broke my magic wand! You wished for a Godparent who could grant wishes?
Lucky boy! Your wish is granted! I'm your Fairy Godfather.

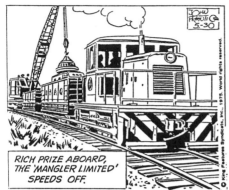

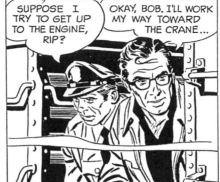

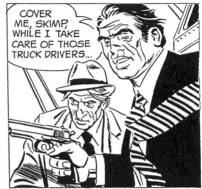

JOHN PRENTICE 5-30
© King Features Syndicate, Inc., 1975. World rights reserved.
RICH PRIZE ABOARD, THE 'MANGLER LIMITED' SPEEDS OFF.
SUPPOSE I TRY TO GET UP TO THE ENGINE, RIP?
OKAY, BOB. I'LL WORK MY WAY TOWARD THE CRANE...
COVER ME, SKIMP, WHILE I TAKE CARE OF THOSE TRUCK DRIVERS...

This episode from *Rip Kirby* is by John Prentice. *Rip Kirby* is one of the most carefully drawn and carefully researched cartoon stories produced today.

of them are pretty odd characters — and odd animals — you will find that there is quite a lot of dialect. It helps to make characters more lively, more interesting.

Some cartoonists mix in a lot of terrible grammar along with the dialect. All kinds of strange sentence construction is used — not at all the sort of thing an English teacher would approve of. For example, in an old comic strip, the cat by the name of Krazy Kat has this to say about his friend Ignatz Mouse:

"Oh, Golla-Golla-
I wunda where about
can Ignatz be at?"

As a friend of Krazy Kat might say, "Ain't this sorta' like awrful poetree?"

OH, GOLLA-GOLLA - I WUNDA WHERE ABOUT CAN 'IGNATZ' BE AT ?

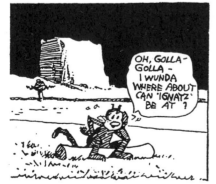

There is another thing that cartoonists do that is very special. It is the use of sound language. It appears in comics where there is a lot of rough and violent action. BAROOMPH! ZAP! KRUNCH! SPLAT! WHOMP! POW! KAKABOOM! Sometimes the lettering used for these words can get really wild.

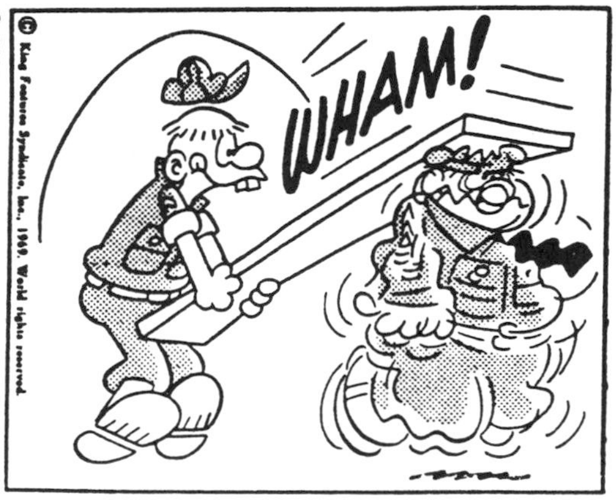
WHAM!

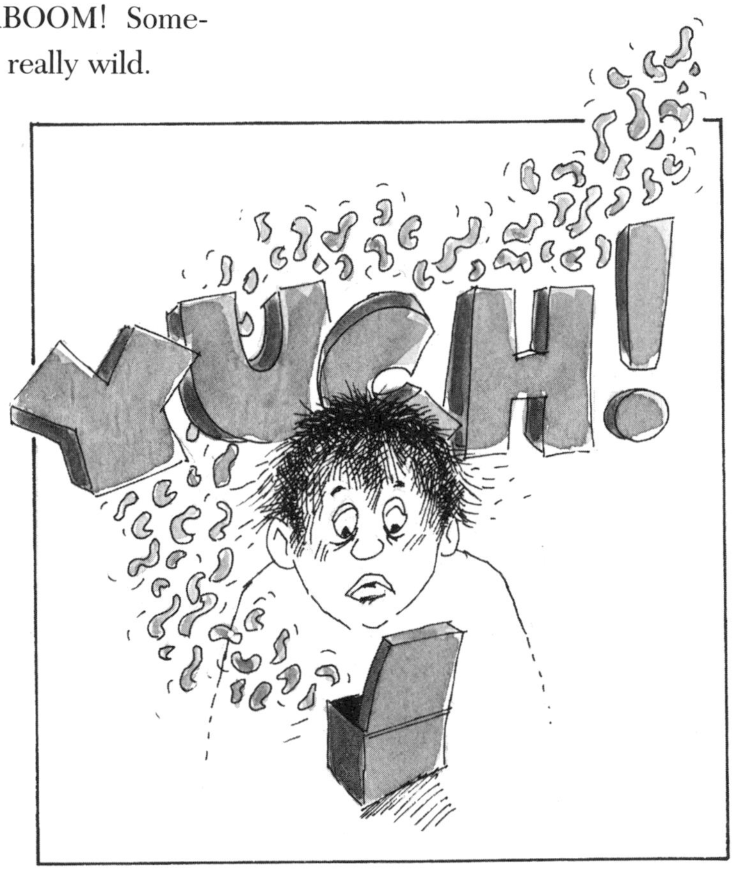
YUCH!

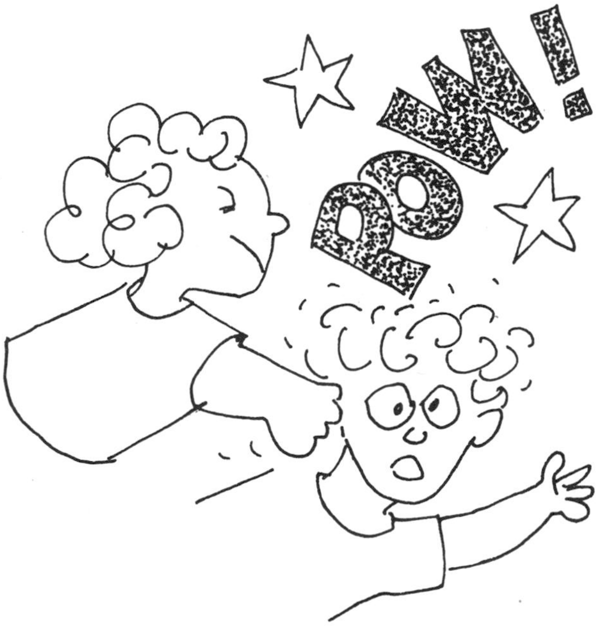
POW!

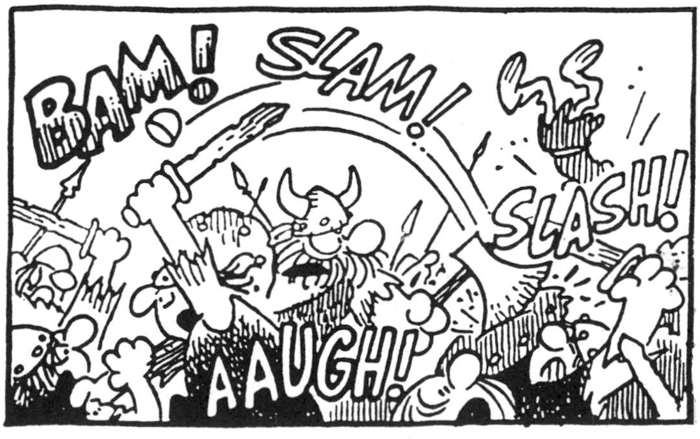
BAM!
SLAM!
SLASH!
AAUGH!

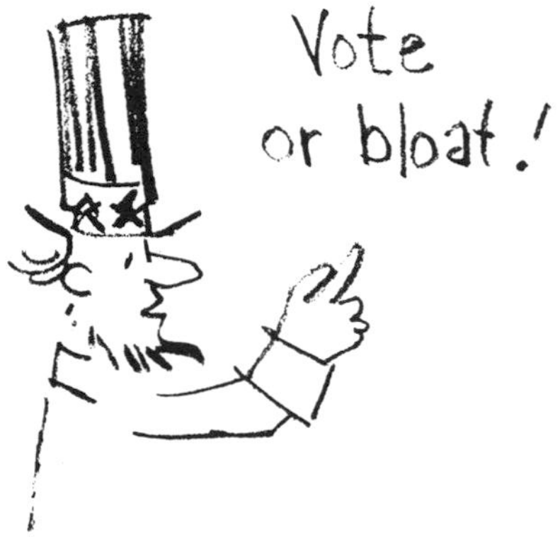
Vote
or bloat!

CARTOONS WITH AN OPINION

A cartoon that expresses an opinion or an idea is called an editorial cartoon. It states the opinion of the artist who draws the cartoon and is just about always in agreement with the political position of the publisher. This kind of cartoon appeared well before anybody ever thought of the gag panel or the comic strip.

The editorial cartoon, if well done, can deal with current-affair problems in an easily understood and dramatic way. It can make a point a lot faster than a long-winded editorial, and it is likely that more people look at the cartoon than read the editorial.

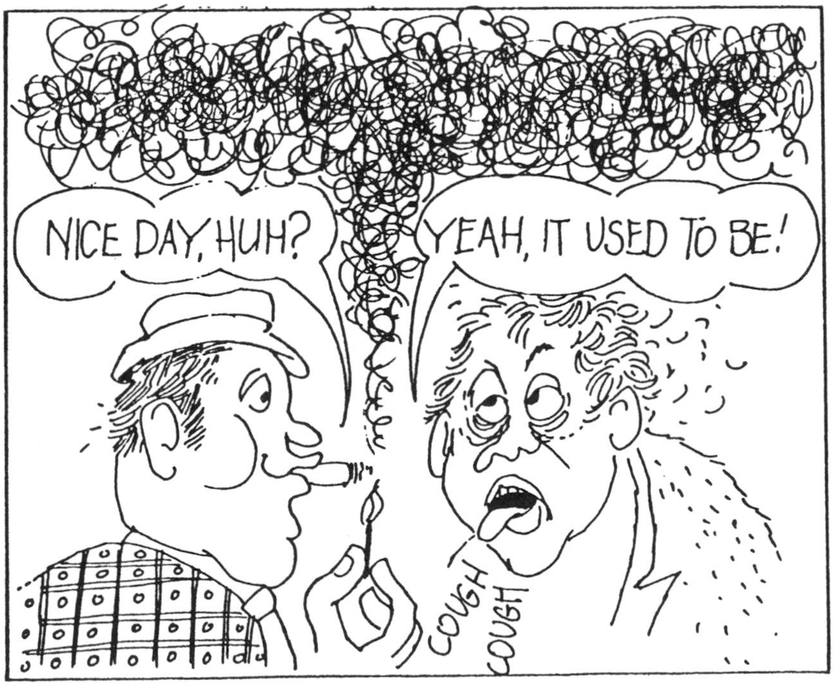
NICE DAY, HUH?
YEAH, IT USED TO BE!
COUGH
COUGH

This cartoonist leaves no doubt in our minds about how he feels about people who smoke cigars in public places!

Uncle Sam is a character that is often found in political cartoons. Whenever a cartoonist wants to say something about government or the state of the union or about the pain of paying taxes he is likely to think of Uncle Sam. That is certainly the case with this cartoon where Uncle Sam is dropping the taxpayers — with money — into one end of the IRS (Internal Revenue Service) and they come out the other end with nothing left but a barrel and a few pennies.

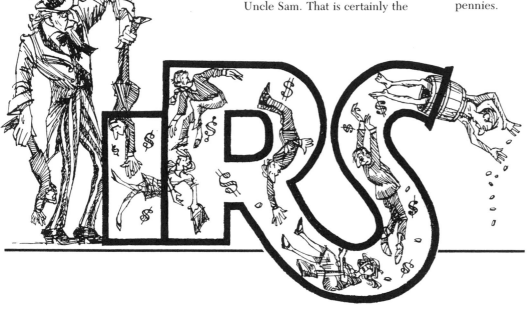

The editorial cartoonist will find all sorts of things to comment about. The problems and worries of the graduating college student is the subject here.

TOTAL FEAR

REPRESENTS $50,000 INVESTMENT

POCKETS EMPTY

KNEES KNOCKING

FEET OF CLAY

EYE TO FUTURE

LUMP IN THROAT

LOTS OF HEART

STOMACH FULL OF BUTTERFLIES

TRANSPORTATION TO MARKET PLACE

FEET TO FALL OVER

HOPE

CASSON

A cartoon can have a message as well as state an opinion. This rather sinister image gives a clear and dramatic warning about the danger of drinking and driving.

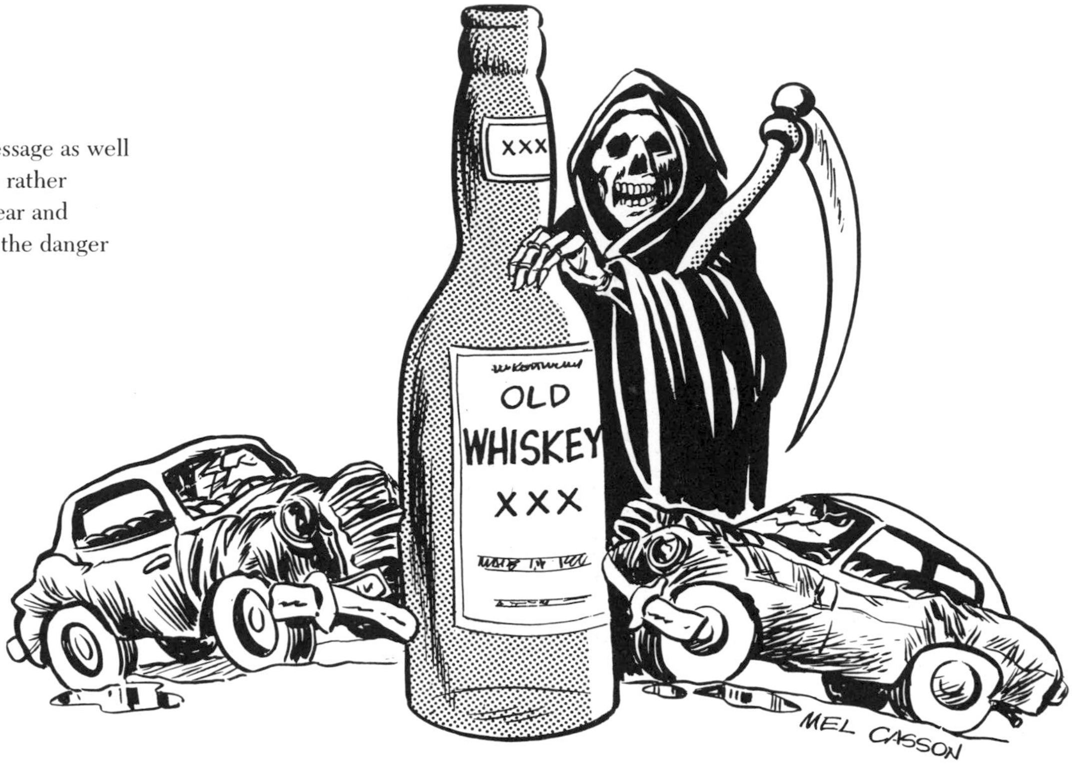
XXX
OLD
WHISKEY
XXX
MEL CASSON

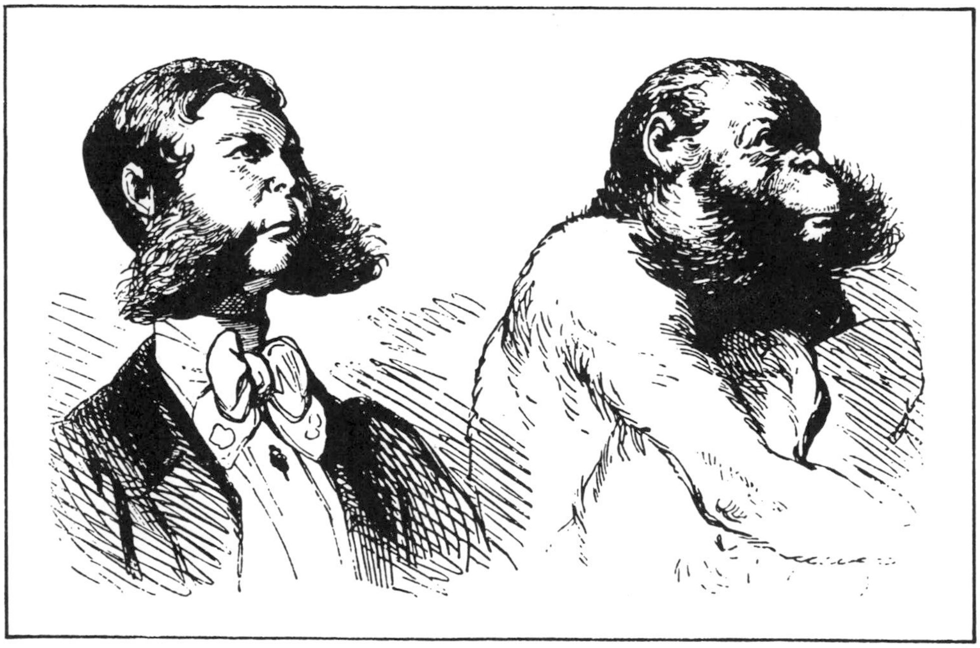

When the beard on a well-dressed dandy is compared with the beard on a rather hairy caveman we know exactly what the cartoonist's opinion is of odd and unlovely beard styles.

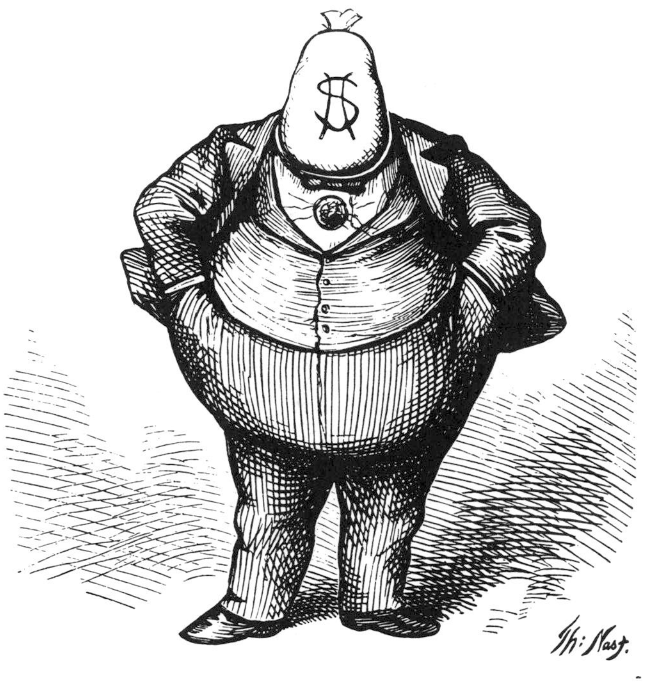
Th: Nast.

This cartoon by Thomas Nast is an example of the kind of thing that a good artist will come up with. It is a famous cartoon which says something — not very complimentary — about Boss Tweed. Boss Tweed ran a political organization in New York City in the 1870s that was rather corrupt. In fact, it was very corrupt. Bribery, cheating, and the misuse of city funds were the scandals of the times. The cartoon shows us the brains behind all this — the grossly overweight Mr. Tweed — a man whose head was filled with thoughts of money and money-making deals.

Political cartoonists deal with day-to-day current events. This cartoon by Bill Yates appeared right after a large pay raise for congressmen was voted down. Notice how the feelings of the characters are shown with the very fewest lines. A good cartoonist can capture mood and action with the simplest drawing.▼

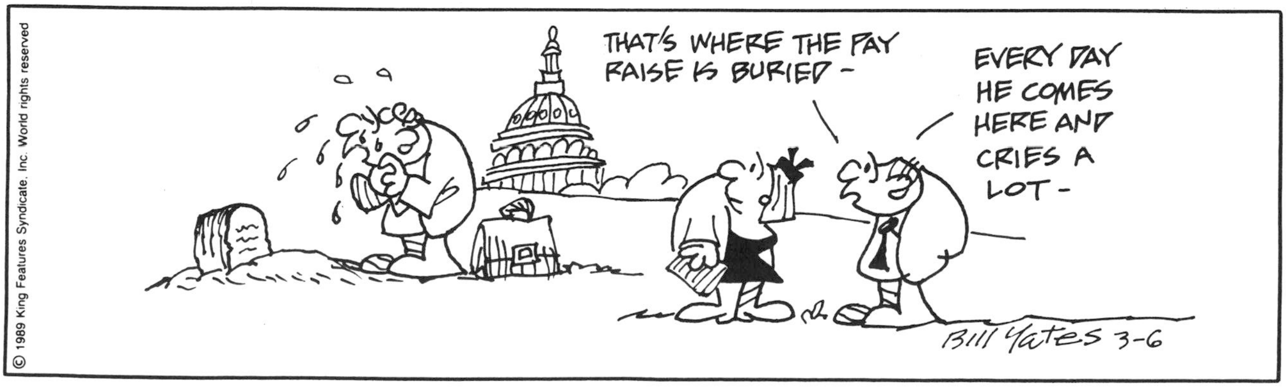
© 1989 King Features Syndicate, Inc. World rights reserved
THAT'S WHERE THE PAY RAISE IS BURIED -
EVERY DAY HE COMES HERE AND CRIES A LOT -
BILL YATES 3-6

The cartoon below was done between the two world wars by George Grosz, an artist who found German military officers something less than attractive. He drew a thoroughly awful character, standing in a sea of wounded bodies, with a bloody sword and a Nazi swastika on his helmet. The rough and jagged style of drawing helps to convey this feeling of cruelty and violence. A drawing like this can be a fine work of art — though it certainly isn't "pretty" — like a sunny landscape or a picture with bright colors and interesting shapes. What it will do is set us thinking. And that is its purpose.

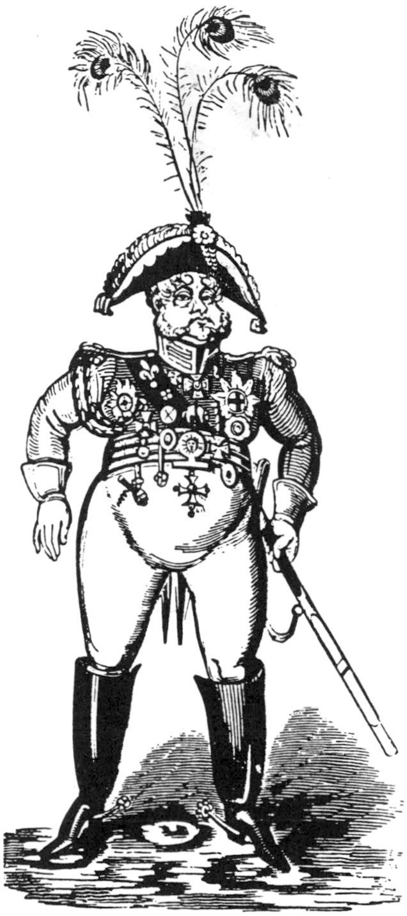

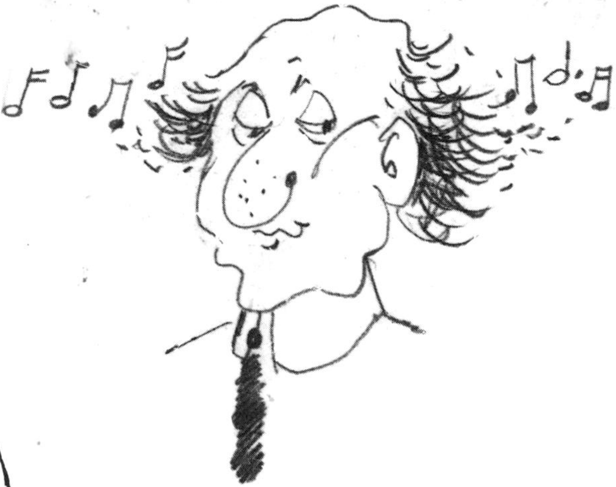

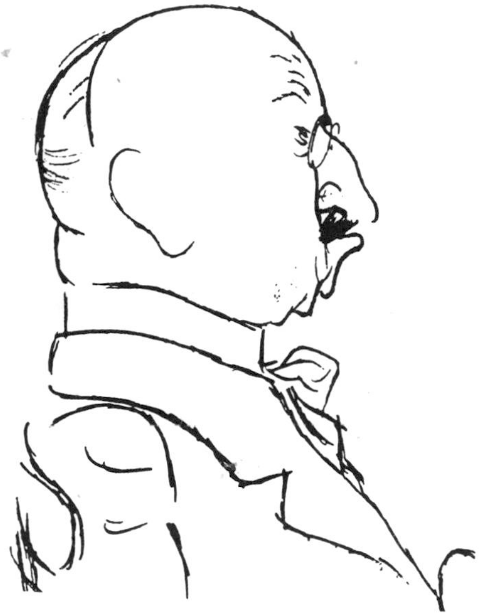

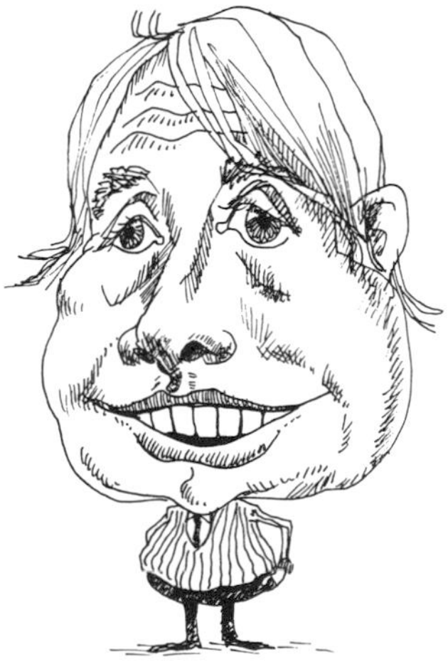

Editorial cartoons often use caricature as a way to make a point or express an opinion. A caricature is a good way to ridicule somebody or something. It is a way to exaggerate an aspect of a person or a situation. If someone has a slightly larger than normal nose, the caricaturist-cartoonist is sure to make it ENORMOUS! If he has large ears they will turn out in the drawing to look huge. In the same way, a political situation that has weak points will have them exaggerated in the most dramatic way.

The editorial cartoonist must be able to draw well. He must have a sense of humor, and he must be very much aware of current events. But most important, he must have the imagination to put his ideas and opinions in a graphic form. That means he must be able to use images rather than words to express himself.

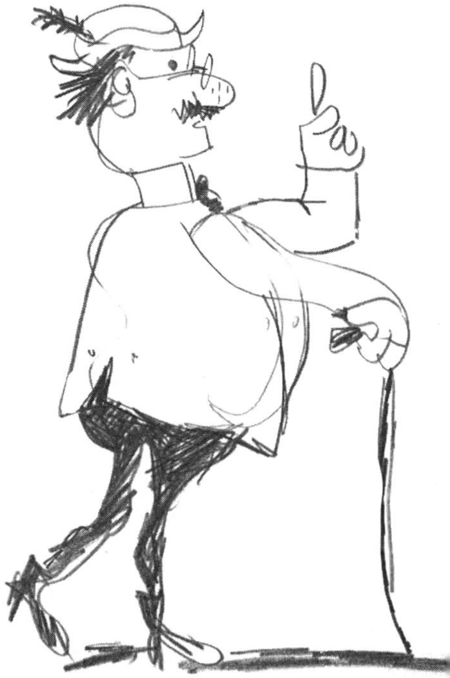

THE ART IN CARTOONS

As you can tell by leafing through the pages of this book, cartoonists draw in many different styles. Some draw in a very realistic way. Others use a simple line drawing and the characters and settings look almost crude. What is important is for the drawing style to suit the subject. In some cartoons the style is

There are as many different styles of drawing as there are cartoonists. Every cartoonist has his own way of working.

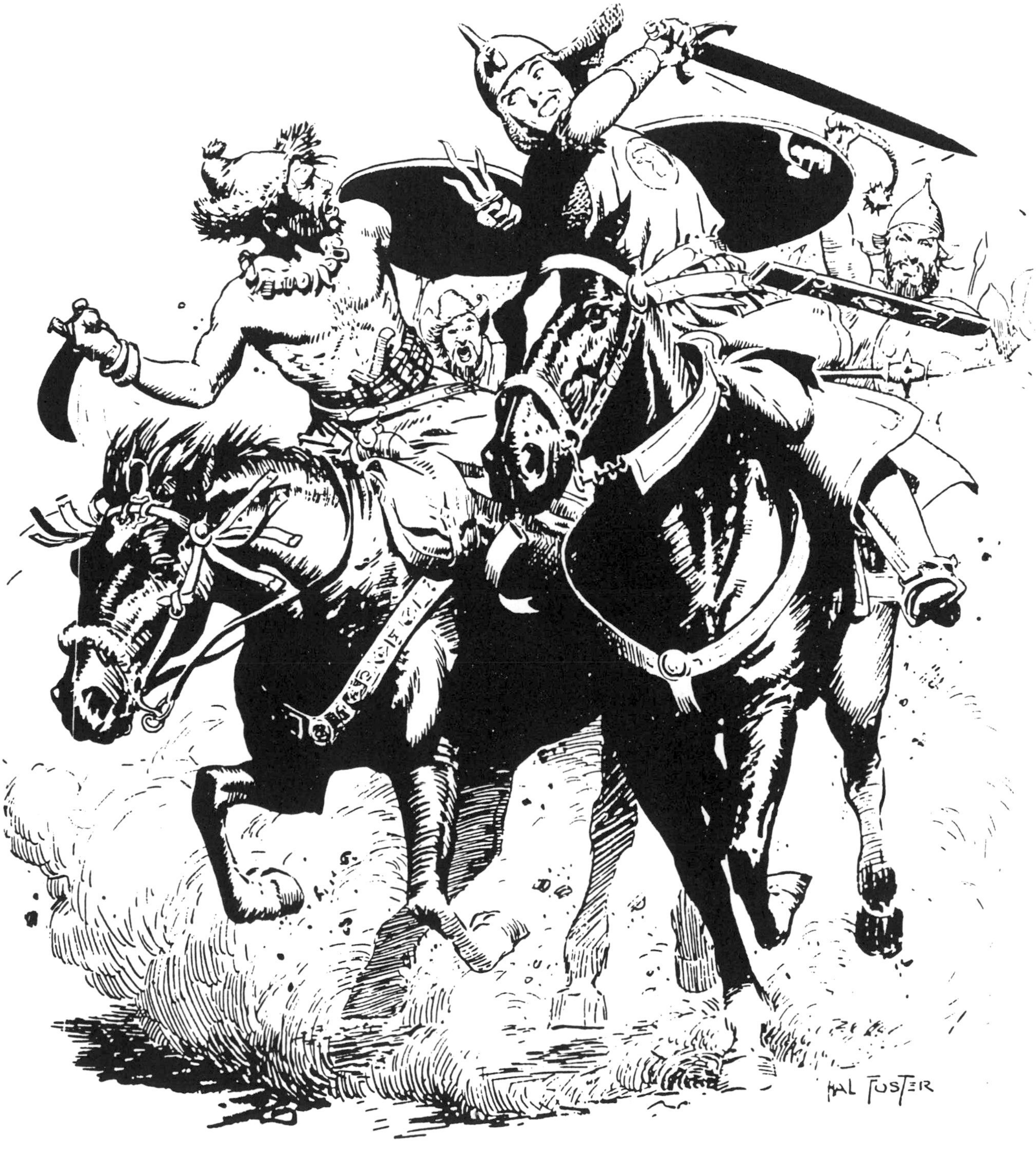
HAL FOSTER

The drawings that illustrate *Prince Valiant* are done with great skill and attention to historical detail. The fierce encounter shown here between Prince Valiant and a knife-wielding enemy is typical of the drawings of Hal Foster, who, for many years did all the illustrations for this story.

very realistic. There are cartoonists who go to great lengths to be sure they have all the details of costume, background, tools, and weapons drawn with exact accuracy. There are other cases where cartoons like *Peanuts* have the very simplest kind of drawing with a minimum of detail and very little in the way of background.

Some cartoons are done with such skill and artistry the drawings are as much fun to look at as the story is to read. The rules that apply to fine art apply to a cartoon strip just as much as to an easel painting or any other work of art. The composition must be carefully designed. There must be variety in tone and texture. The important action must be given the proper emphasis. All these things must be in the mind of the cartoonist as well as the written part of the cartoon. This is one of the reasons some cartoonists think of themselves as being in some ways superior to other artists. After all, they are drawing pictures and at the same time writing a story. They are author and artist all in one.

Most cartoonists are skilled draftsmen who have studied art for years. Some of them started out to be serious painters but decided at some point that cartoons are more fun, or more challenging and usually much better paid. There were many artists, particularly in the 19th century, who were serious painters as well as cartoonists.

The difference between fine art, illustration, and cartoons is sometimes blurred. We think of fine artists as standing in front of their easels and painting whatever they want. An illustrator is thought of as someone who is paid to illustrate a story or product, and we assume a cartoonist's job is to dream up funny situations or draw political comments. But the differences aren't always clear.

The cartoonist or illustrator might do work that some people consider fine art. And the fine artist might do work that illustrates an idea or a story. So labels must be applied with care — or sometimes, perhaps, avoided altogether.

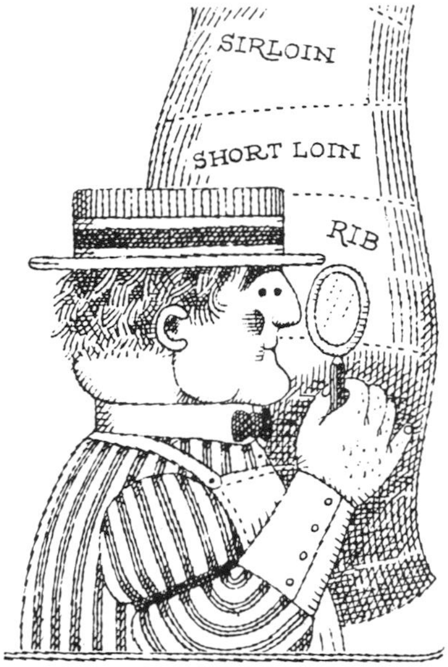
SIRLOIN
SHORT LOIN
RIB

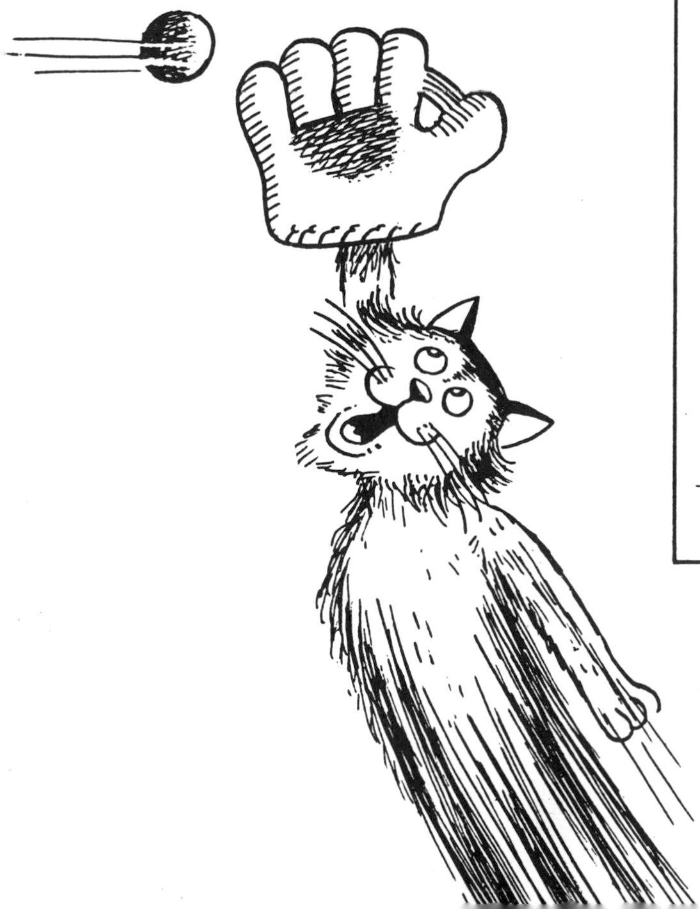

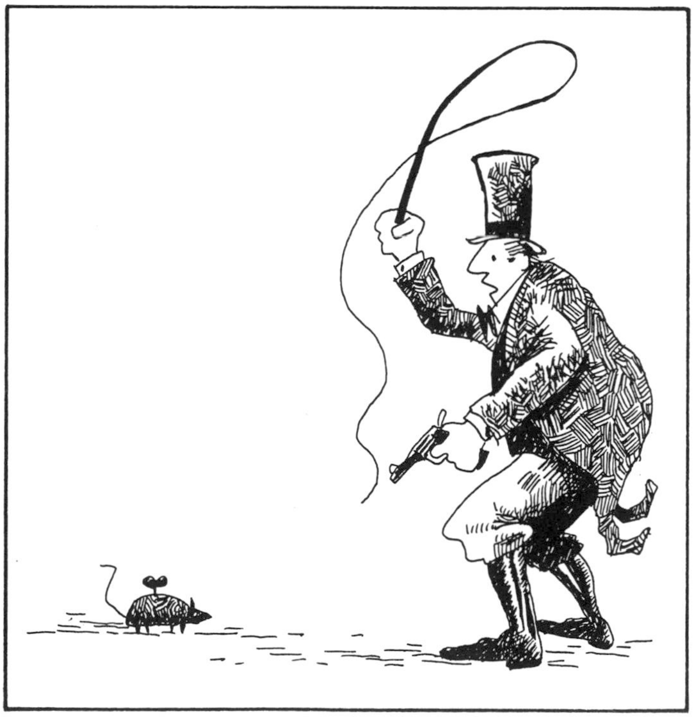

Many artists, illustrators, and cartoonists like to draw with pen and ink. The drawing on this and the facing page were all done this way.

I guess you're right, Ellen. However it happened, it's all over now . . . And all's well that ends well . . . So let's–
What was that?
Past the window! . . . A large bird— Where's Barnaby?

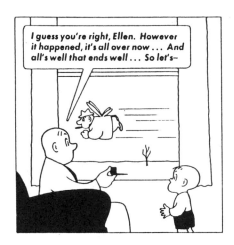

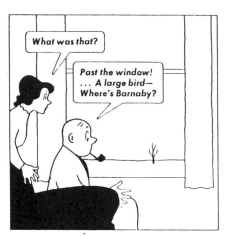

The drawing style used by Crockett Johnson to tell the story of Barnaby and his fairy godfather is quite simple. There is no shading, and the backgrounds are uncluttered. Even the lettering has a mechanical look. That is because the text has been set in type, rather than lettered by hand. Practically all cartoonists letter in their text by hand, however.

The way newspapers are printed has a good deal to say about how a cartoonist can work. Delicate shading and subtle colors won't print well. The very fast printing press and coarse paper permit only flat tones and plain lines. The Sunday comics are printed in color because this section is printed separately from the rest of the paper. But if you look carefully you will see that the basic drawing is in black line. The color is added over the line drawing. It is a little like the way you might add watercolor over a drawing you did with pencil or pen and ink.

When a cartoonist wants to get a gray tone in a drawing he sometimes uses something called a benday. It is a pattern of dots, which can be placed on the drawing where needed. The cartoonist whose work will be printed in a magazine has much more freedom. Magazines are printed more carefully and on a much better grade of paper. Soft, shaded tones and delicate lines are possible.

This is a drawing by Bud Sagendorf, who has drawn *Popeye* for many years. Part of it is shown in the size it was actually drawn. And below, it is shown reduced to the size it would appear in most newspapers. Just about all cartoonists make their drawings larger than the final printed size. A big drawing makes it easier to get all the details right. It is also simpler to make changes.

Notice that there is an even pattern of dots in the pants of the poor fellow Popeye is pounding on. This pattern of dots — called a benday — is printed on a thin sheet of plastic that is cut to the desired shape and then stuck onto the drawing. When the drawing is reduced in size the dots blend to form a gray tone. This is a common method that many cartoonists use to get a little tonal variety in their drawings.

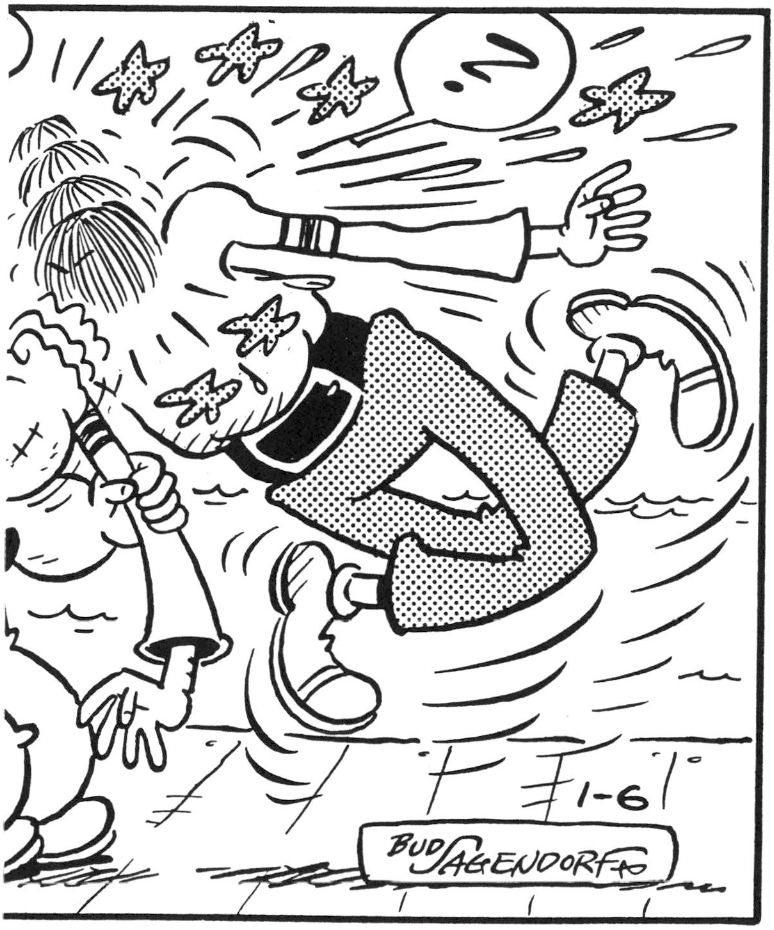
?
1-6
BUD SAGENDORF

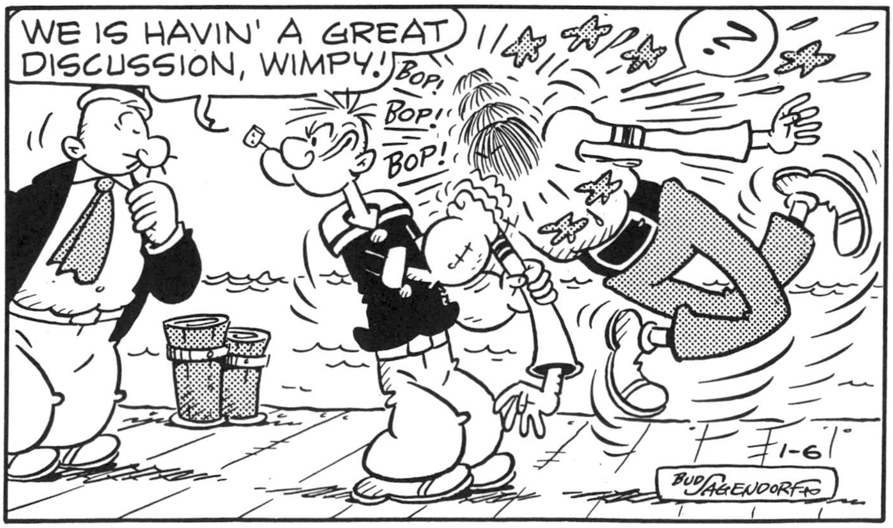
WE IS HAVIN' A GREAT DISCUSSION, WIMPY!
BOP!
BOP!
BOP!
?
1-6
BUD SAGENDORF

THE CARTOON BUSINESS

There are certain organizations that handle all the complicated details involved in the production and distribution of cartoons. When a cartoon strip is very popular, like *Peanuts* or *Blondie* or *Beetle Bailey*, it may appear in over a thousand newspapers all around the world. The companies that take care of all this arranging and keeping track are called syndicates. They represent the cartoonist and protect his rights. They arrange schedules and make sure the cartoons get to the right place at the right time. Another very important thing they do is produce and sell all the side products of the cartoon. The syndicates will publish a collection of the cartoons in book or magazine form. They will arrange for the production of toys or shirts or posters that show the cartoon's characters. You can walk into many toy stores and buy a small statue or toy figure of Snoopy or Mickey Mouse or Superman and quite a few other characters who first saw the light of day in a daily comic strip. All this sort of thing is handled by syndicates.

For the cartoonist trying to get a start, the first and most urgent task is to find a syndicate that will take him on. Once the cartoonist is represented by a syndicate the job of sales and promotion is in the hands of specialists, and his career is off to a good start.

Most cartoonists do all the writing and drawing themselves. But there are others who work as part of a team. One person may be the writer and another will draw the pictures. This is the usual case with comic books that are published frequently and have many pages. The team can, in fact, be fairly large. There will be an editor or general supervisor, the writer, and one or two people who do the drawings in pencil. Then there will be someone to ink in the pencil drawings, a letterer, someone to take care of the color, and one or two more people who deal with all the other odds and ends.

When a cartoonist dies or retires a comic strip is sometimes abandoned. This happens if the drawing and writing are so distinctive that nobody else is able to carry it on. But in many cases the strip is taken over by another cartoonist. If the readers are so attached to a strip that they demand it continue, the syndicate will find somebody to take it over. Sometimes there may be several people who will work on one comic strip over a period of years. This has happened with *Little Orphan Annie, Blondie, Prince Valiant*, and many others. *Little Orphan Annie*, for example, has been in existence since 1924, and during that time many different people have worked on it. It is still going strong with pretty much the same characters and pretty much the same drawing style.

ANIMATED CARTOONS

Cartoons appear not only in newspapers, magazines, and comic books. They also come to life on the movie or TV screen. An animated film is made with many drawings, each drawing changed slightly from the one before. If a cartoon film were being made of the clown above jumping out of the ink bottle there would be a great many more drawings, with the change from one position to the next being much more gradual.

Each drawing is photographed by a movie camera — one frame at a time. The film is then projected at a speed of 16 frames a second. When the drawings are shown on the screen at this speed the eye cannot separate one from another. They blend together and there is smooth and continuous motion.

The animated-cartoon maker uses many filming tricks to get varied backgrounds and different kinds of motion. All sorts of realistic or wild and unrealistic action are possible. Snow White can walk gracefully along a beautiful forest path. Or Donald Duck can drop off the edge of a cliff, tumble down two miles, bounce back up, and land on a cloud. Realism or fantasy are both possible.

There is a lot of give-and-take between the comic strip and the animated movie cartoon. Sometimes a character like Mickey Mouse will first appear as a movie character. Then, because he is so popular, he will be used in a comic strip. The opposite of this has also happened. Superman started as a comic-strip character and has been made into several movies.

Walt Disney is the most famous name in animated-cartoon films. He started his career with black-and-white films that lasted only a few minutes. But as his skills developed, so did the films.

© 1990 KFS, Inc.

When a character is used in an animated film his or her appearance must not change when different artists at different times do the drawing. Therefore, standard drawings like this one of Felix the Cat are used as reference. This way Felix will always look exactly the same, year after year, even though drawn by many different artists. These reference drawings are called "model sheets."

Eventually he produced full-color, feature-length films that were ambitious productions with exciting settings, dramatic characters, and impressive musical scores.. Some of these films, which you have probably seen, are *Snow White and the Seven Dwarfs*, *Pinocchio*, *Fantasia*, as well as many others.

EYE BROWS HEAVY
KEEP COLLAR LARGE
3 STRIPES ON JERSEY
SINDBAD THE SAILOR
SASH BOW ON RIGHT SIDE

P83
THE GOON

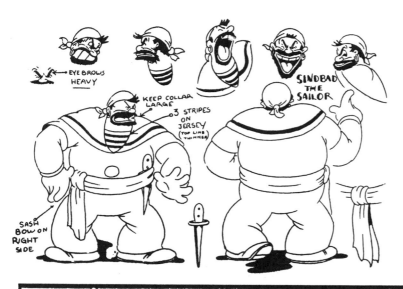

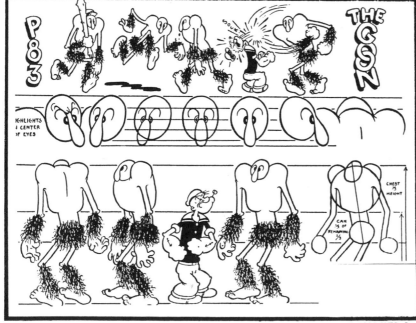

These two model sheets show the proportions and gestures of two of the rough-and-ready characters that appeared in many *Popeye* animated films. The facial expressions of Sindbad the Sailor are shown — everything from a friendly grin to a fierce scowl, and his suit is shown from front and back.

The facial expressions of the Goon are also shown in the lower model sheet. But they are rather limited, which is understandable, since there are no ears, mouth, or eyebrows to deal with. However, the rather strange location and arrangement of the hair is shown in very clear detail!

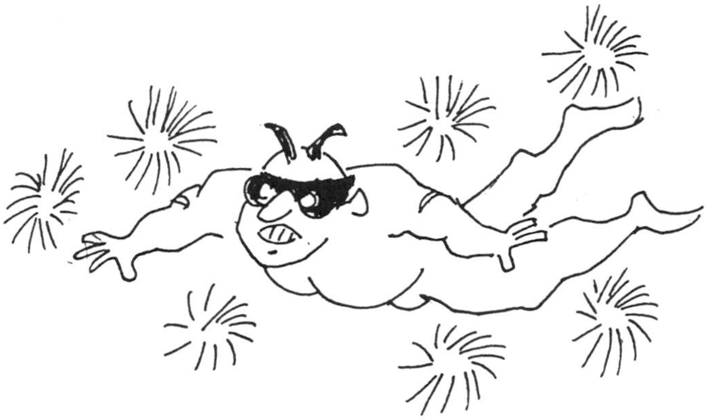

COMIC BOOKS

The comic book isn't really a book, and it isn't often comical. It is like a very long comic strip that goes on for many pages. Most comic books deal with one particular character — Batman, the Incredible Hulk, Spider-man, Popeye, or any of the other cartoon heroes that appear in the daily or Sunday comic pages. There are also other comic books with original adventure and fantasy fiction written and drawn only for comic-book publication.

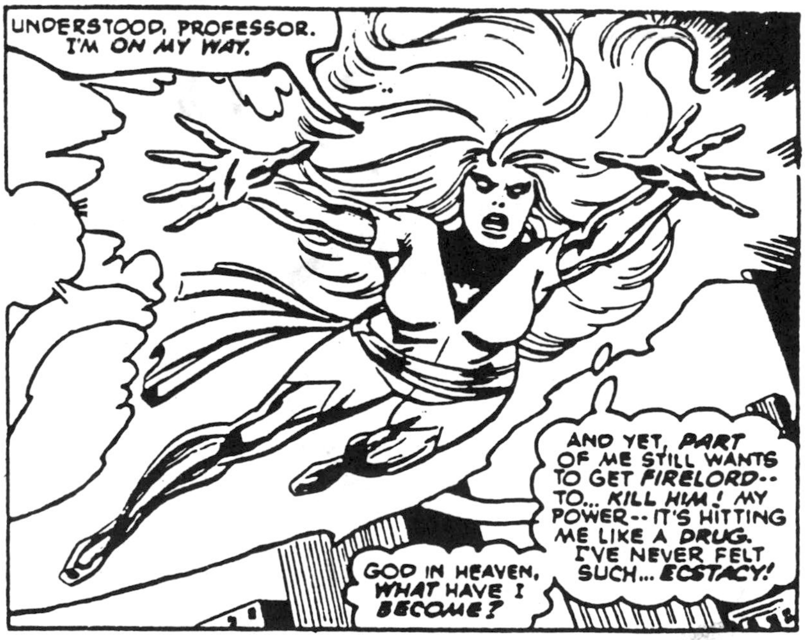
UNDERSTOOD, PROFESSOR. I'M ON MY WAY.
GOD IN HEAVEN, WHAT HAVE I BECOME?
AND YET, PART OF ME STILL WANTS TO GET FIRELORD-- TO... KILL HIM! MY POWER-- IT'S HITTING ME LIKE A DRUG. I'VE NEVER FELT SUCH... ECSTACY!

Very few science-fiction comic-book characters simply walk or run from one place to another. There is a great deal of flying around, as in this panel where the heroine is off on a mysterious mission of some sort.

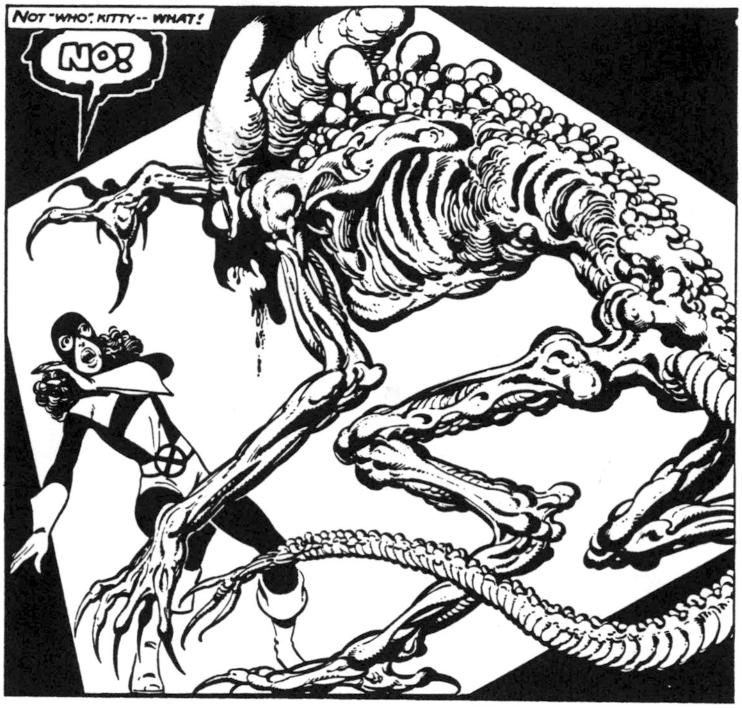
NOT "WHO", KITTY -- WHAT!
NO!

There is nothing like a huge, bony, disgusting monster like this to liven up the action on an imaginary distant planet!

Some comic books come out monthly, like magazines. Often the "bad guys" appear and reappear and get to be as well known as the hero characters. The usual comic book is about thirty-two pages long and unfortunately is printed on a poor-quality paper. But even so, they are collected by a great many people. Some collectors have hundreds or thousands of comic books. Many of the rare old ones are quite valuable, selling for a good deal of money, and there are comic-book fairs where there is much trading back and forth, as well as a lot of buying and selling.

Comic books are longer and more complex than the single comic strip or gag-panel cartoons and they require a fairly elaborate team — writer, artists, letterers, and others. After a while the serious comic-book reader gets to know the work and style of these different people. Some collectors prefer one particular artist or writer and concentrate on gathering as much of his work as possible.

The unreal, science-fiction world of the future has always been a major interest of comic-book authors, artists, and their readers of all ages. There are all kinds of tales of exotic places and people, strange animals, and fantastic mutants from planets light years away. The pages are full of space vehicles shooting back and forth

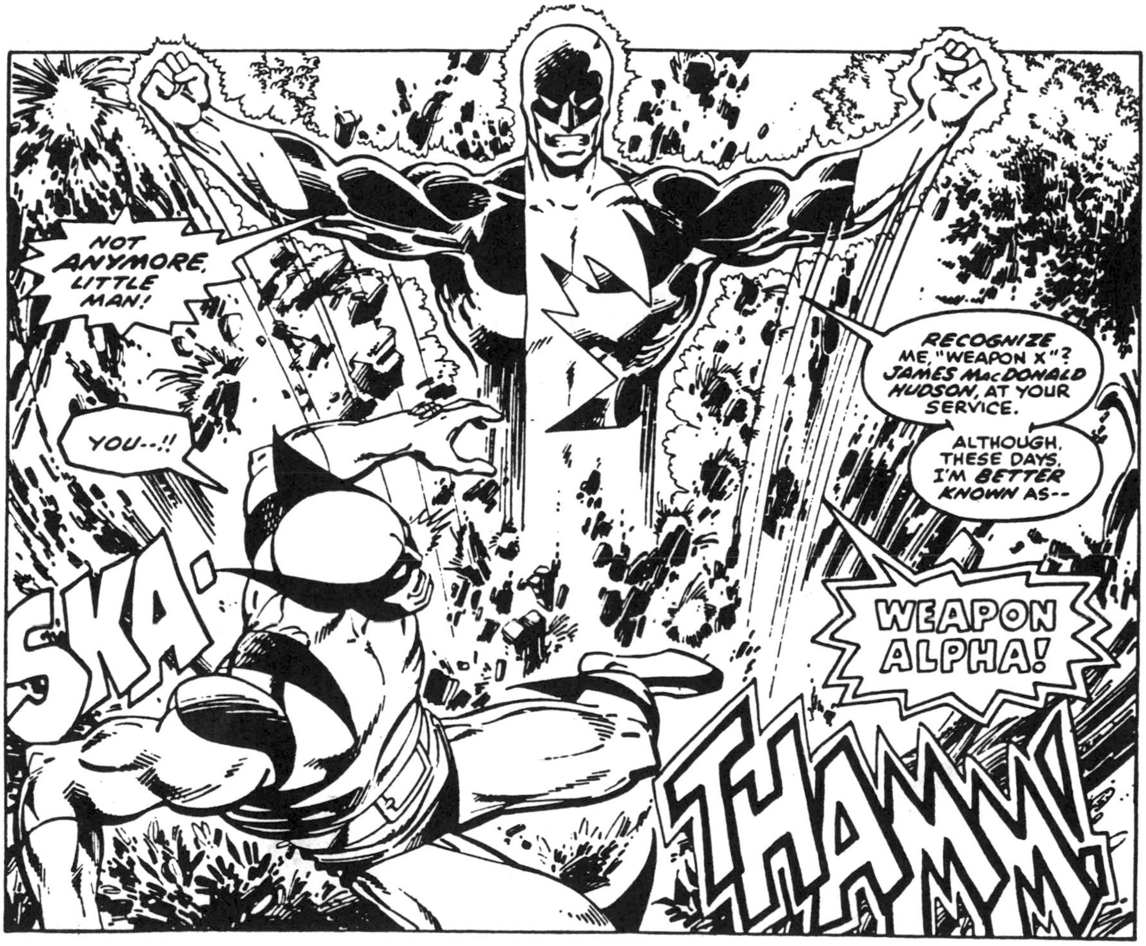
NOT ANYMORE, LITTLE MAN!
YOU--!!
RECOGNIZE ME, "WEAPON X"? JAMES MacDONALD HUDSON, AT YOUR SERVICE.
ALTHOUGH, THESE DAYS, I'M BETTER KNOWN AS--
WEAPON ALPHA!
SKA-
THAMM!

In the land of fantasy adventure the drawing is usually busy, slam-bang, and filled to the brim with all kinds of detail. This drawing, done many years ago by John Byrne, one of the best-known comic-book artists, is typical. There is hardly any empty space. There are two figures, clouds of smoke, flying bits and pieces from an explosion — all this plus scattered conversation and a big SKA-THAMM!, and all contained in one panel. Yet, because of the skill of the artist the action is quite clear and everything seems to belong in place.

Comic-book villains can be really terrible. They are over-muscled, scary-looking, and able to destroy buildings, enslave children, and do every awful thing you can think of — the more awful the better! ▼

Popular cartoon characters and comic strips will, as a rule, eventually turn up as a collection in book form. The page opposite is from a book of several hundred pages that contains *Hägar the Horrible* cartoons that were published over many years. ▶

in intergalactic space while strange creatures hatch sinister plots. Some comic-book people like Superman, Batman, Spider-man, and The Hulk exist in present-day times but manage to perform all sorts of unbelievable and fantastic actions.

But there are mixed opinions about comic books. A lot of people don't think too much of them. Comic books are so easy to read that some people read nothing else — and never sit down with more serious, worthwhile books. There are also objections to those comic books which show cruel and violent behavior. In some comic books there are savage murders, shootings, knifings, beatings, torture! Terrible gross and ugly goings-on! Now all of this is, of course, not realistic — even if the drawings are. It is wild, imaginative fantasy and not to be taken seriously. But the critics of this kind of comic book say that making violence of this kind appear usual and normal will make it more acceptable in ordinary day-to-day life.

But, fortunately, most comic books are not like this. Most tell exciting adventure tales or stories set in fantastic other-world civilizations. And there are comic books full of good humor and funny situations. Some of them deal with characters like Hägar the Horrible on the facing page — who is more funny than horrible. And there are comic books with Donald Duck, Dick Tracy, Blondie, Peanuts, Calvin and Hobbes, and many other funny characters.

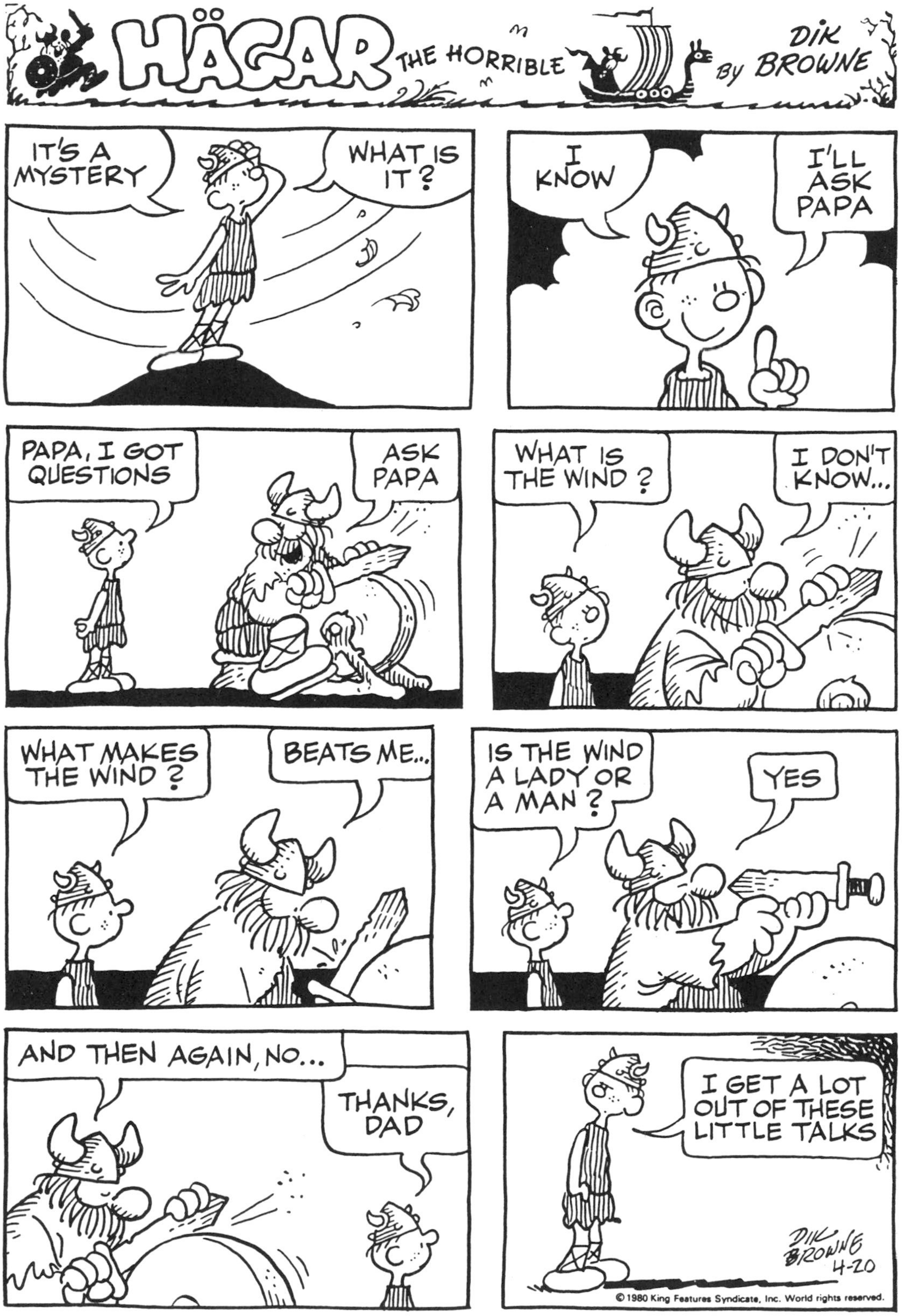
HÄGAR THE HORRIBLE
BY DIK BROWNE
IT'S A MYSTERY
WHAT IS IT?
I KNOW
I'LL ASK PAPA
PAPA, I GOT QUESTIONS
ASK PAPA
WHAT IS THE WIND?
I DON'T KNOW...
WHAT MAKES THE WIND?
BEATS ME...
IS THE WIND A LADY OR A MAN?
YES
AND THEN AGAIN, NO...
THANKS, DAD
I GET A LOT OUT OF THESE LITTLE TALKS
DIK BROWNE 4-20
© 1980 King Features Syndicate, Inc. World rights reserved.

Comic books are to be found almost everywhere. They appear in different languages all over the world. The American comic books will have a different language dubbed in when they are printed for sale in foreign lands. There are also many comic books that originate in other countries. Japanese comic books are very popular there, and the French produce many colorful, lurid ones. But the biggest selection and most varied types come from the United States.

Some comic books actually are books, not the flimsy, poorly printed thirty-two-page types. These better-quality cartoon books are often printed in black and white, are quite long, and contain cartoons that originally appeared in newspapers. In many cases, they are collections of comics that are very popular and worth saving. They vary, of course, some of them being quite elegant, printed on good paper, and costing a lot more than the common, thin comic book. Sometimes they are called collections rather than comic books and are a different matter altogether.

Imaginary landscapes peopled by creatures from outer space are a specialty of some comic-book artists. These drawings are fantastic, wild, and filled with all kinds of surprising details.

DOING IT YOURSELF

If you have a few bright ideas, a little imagination, and a sense of humor — everybody has — then there is no reason you can't make some kind of comic strip of your own!

Drawing skill is, of course, something that would be nice to have, but it isn't absolutely essential. It is possible to make a comic strip using only the simplest stick figures or uncomplicated geometric shapes. Don't forget that the cartoonist is a writer as well as an artist. You may want to concentrate on the written or idea part. Or you might decide to collaborate with a friend — each of you doing the thing you do best. With luck, one of you would be the artist, the other the writer.

Here are a few hints that should help you get started:

Begin with a character. Funny-looking people, odd clothing, talking animals, outer-space creatures — these are great fun and will give you something to start with.

Simple geometric shapes will help you build the sort of figures you want. The shape of a head can be easily made with a circle or an oval.

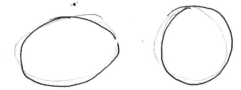

Eyes can be dots or small circles or arcs.

Here are some noses.

The mouth can be drawn in many different ways and has a lot to do with facial expression.

There are many additional details that can give a more interesting or realistic look.

The head when viewed from the side — in profile — is drawn a little differently, and gives you a chance to have some fun experimenting with noses — all sizes and shapes! Cartoonists love to draw big, fancy noses.

A backward or forward *C* makes a good-looking ear.

Hair is easy to make. Mustaches, beards, as well as long and fancy hair styles, will make a head a lot more interesting.

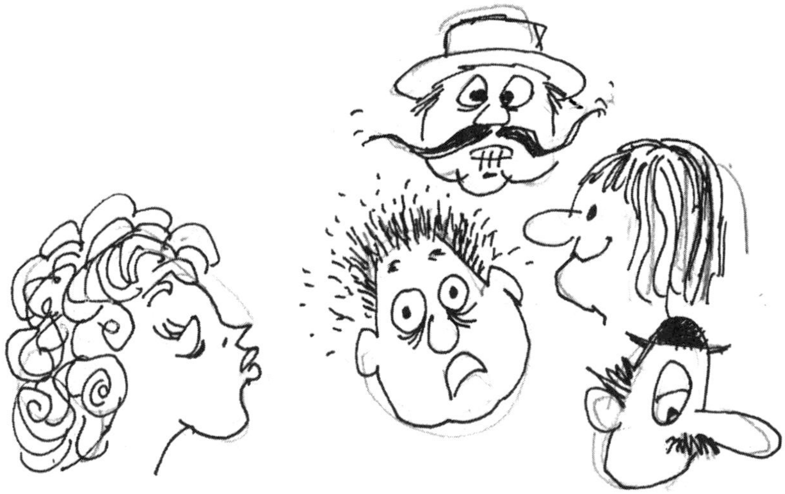

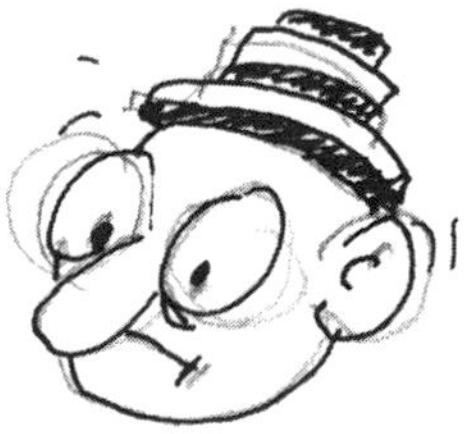

Try drawing heads with all kinds of expressions — happy, sad, surprised, angry, puzzled, curious, smart — whatever you can think of.

The body is basically an oval shape that can be altered to suit the sort of character you want to draw.

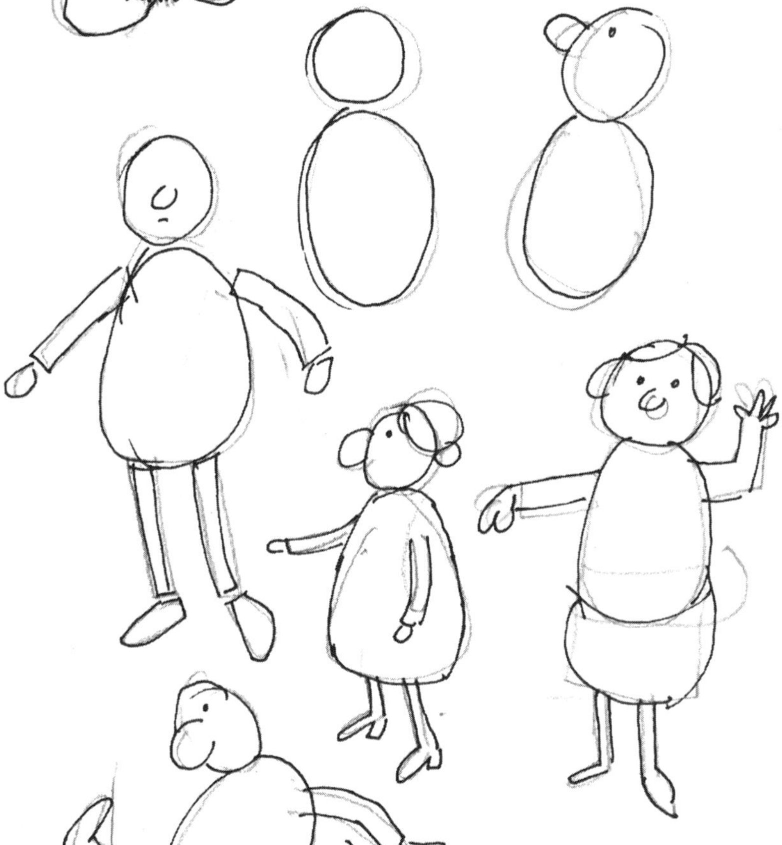

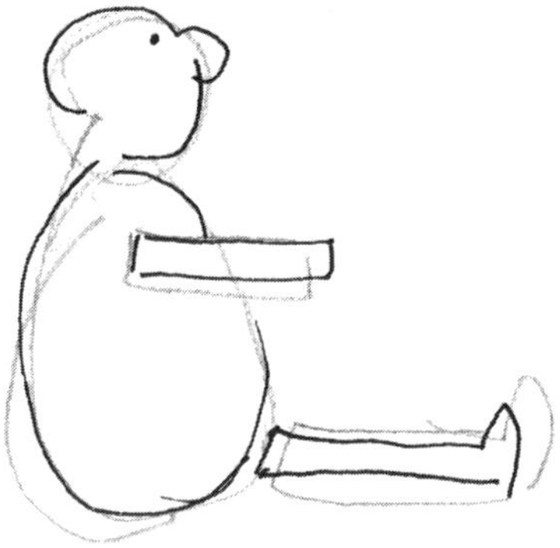

Arms and legs can be drawn most easily as long, thin rectangles. All of this is, of course, a matter of personal preference. An artist is permitted — and expected — to do things his own way!

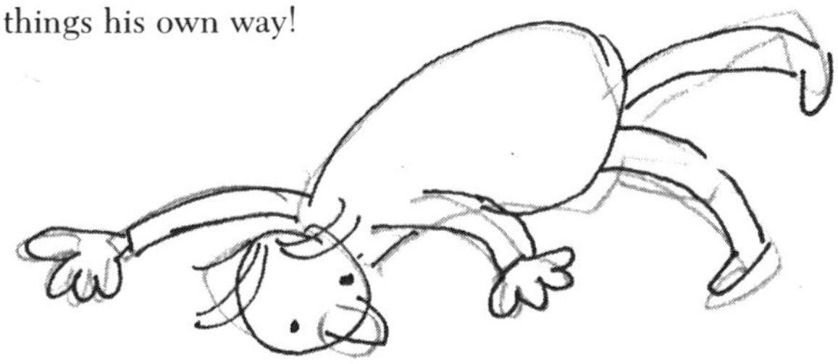

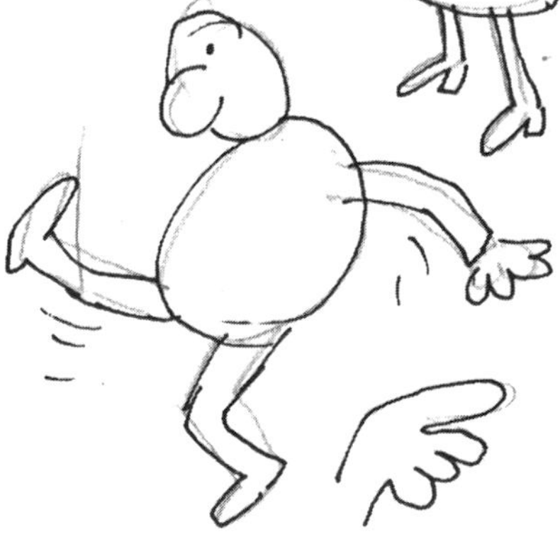

Hands, which are not easy to draw, can be done in many different ways. Many cartoonists make quick, sketchy-looking hands with only four fingers!

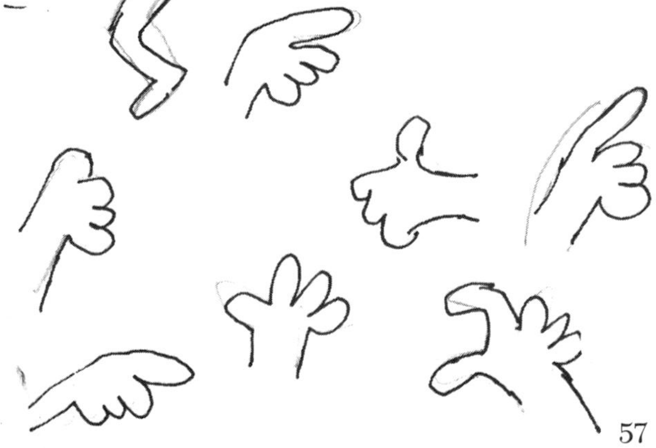

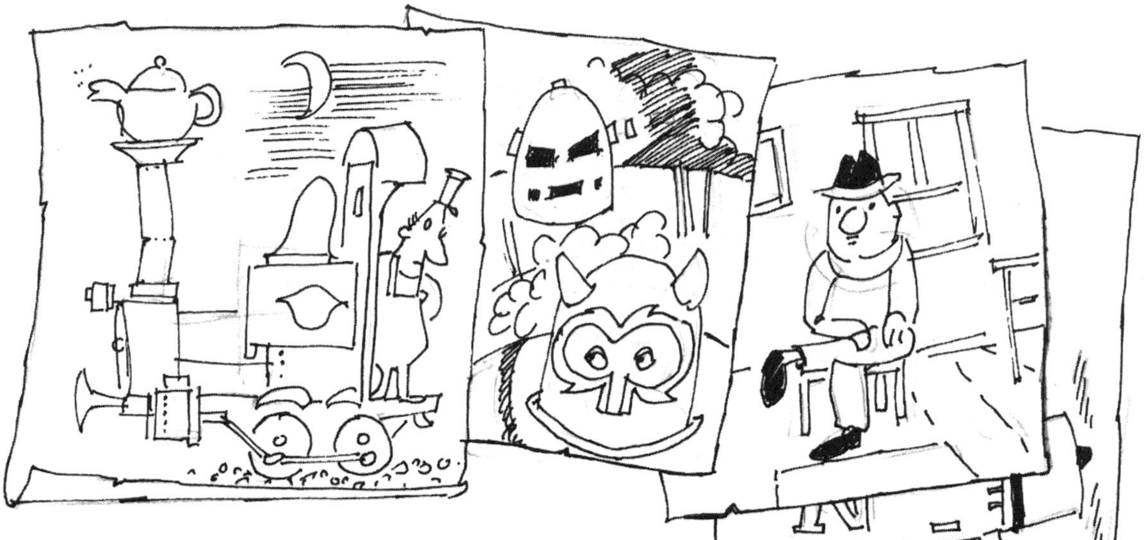

Learning to draw cartoons, or anything, is a matter of practice, practice, and more practice. The more, the better. You can practice by copying the published cartoons that you like or by drawing the objects and people around you.▲

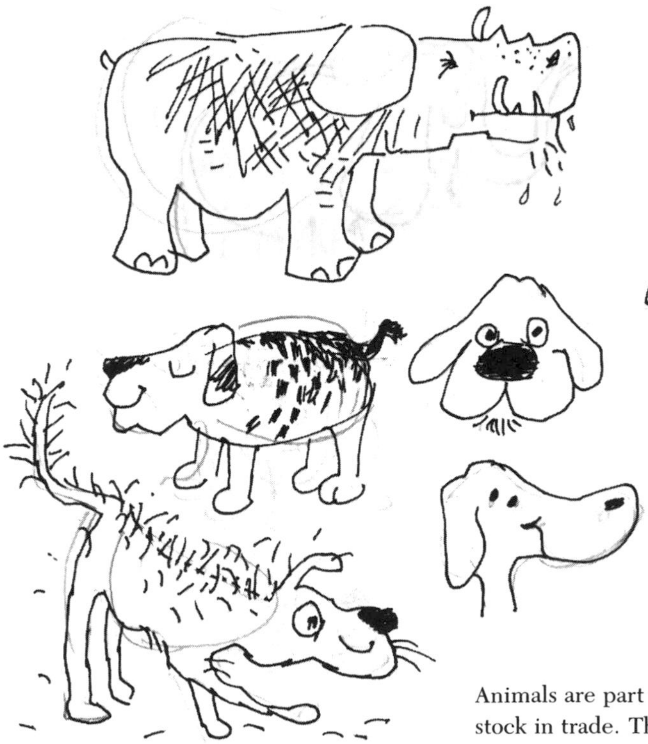

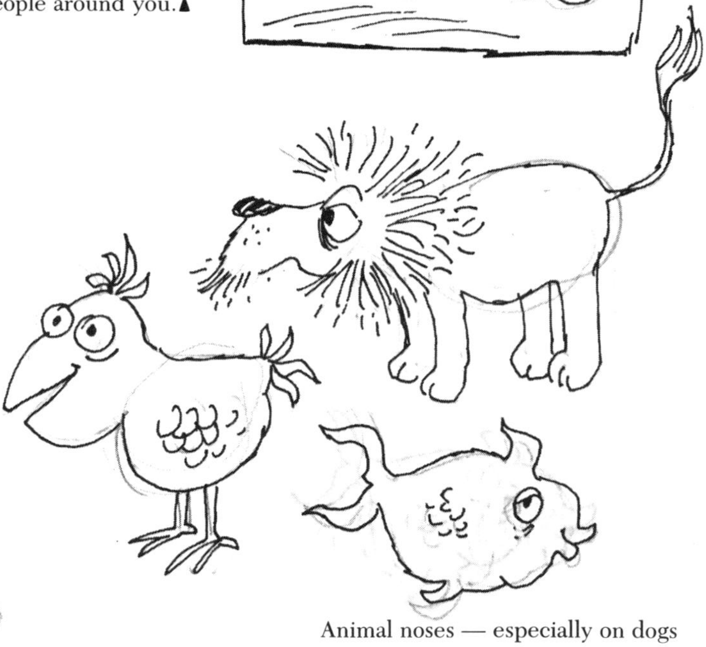

Animal noses — especially on dogs and cats — are usually big black circles. Ears come in all sizes and shapes. Dots, dashes, and smudges will show marking on the skin, or fur.▲

Animals are part of the cartoonist's stock in trade. They can be drawn with the combination of circles and ovals that are used for drawing people.

As a cartoonist you can make people shrink, houses fly, ice-cream cones explode, clouds turn into polka-dotted spacecraft — whatever, however you want. You don't have to worry about practical matters. Ideas and imagination are the important things. Common sense and the laws of nature don't concern most cartoonists. However, there is no reason you can't tell a realistic story with real people, if that is what you want to do.

No special tools are needed to draw cartoons. Anything that will leave a mark can be used — pencil, pen, or brush and ink, crayon, charcoal, even the computer.

Many good ideas for cartoons start as a simple doodle — strange faces, odd objects, peculiar combinations of things. If you find it hard to begin, try doodling and see what happens . . .

If you want to make a cartoon strip — comic or an adventure story, or whatever — just jump in and get started! Don't worry about long-range planning or what is going to happen later on. Starting is the hardest part. Once you've started, one thing will suggest another and you will be on your way. A good trick to get yourself started is to make a title panel, or a title page. Even if it doesn't have much to do with anything, and you have only the foggiest notion of what is going to happen, it will be a beginning, and that is what is important!

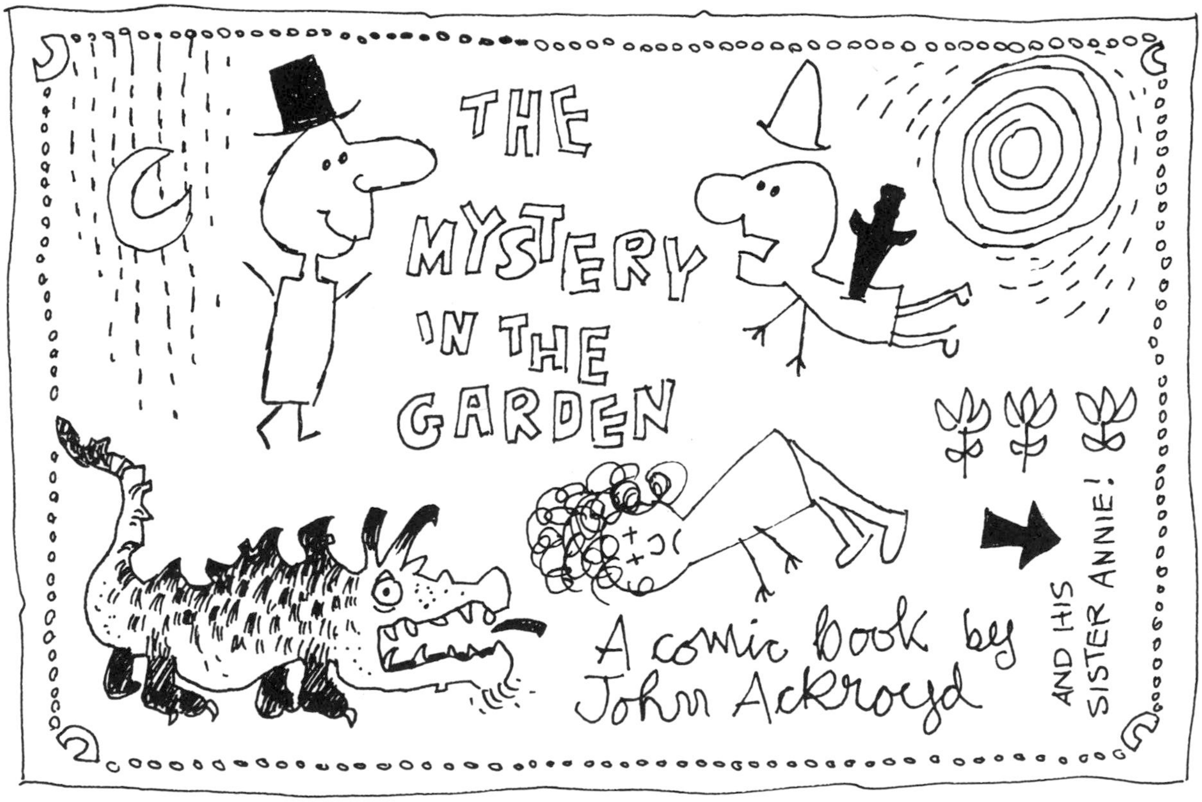
THE MYSTERY IN THE GARDEN
A comic book by John Ackroyd
AND HIS SISTER ANNIE!

If you like funny cartoons or gag panels and want to make some of your own you must be constantly on the lookout for suitable ideas. Often, something that has happened to you or your friends and relatives will provide an idea.

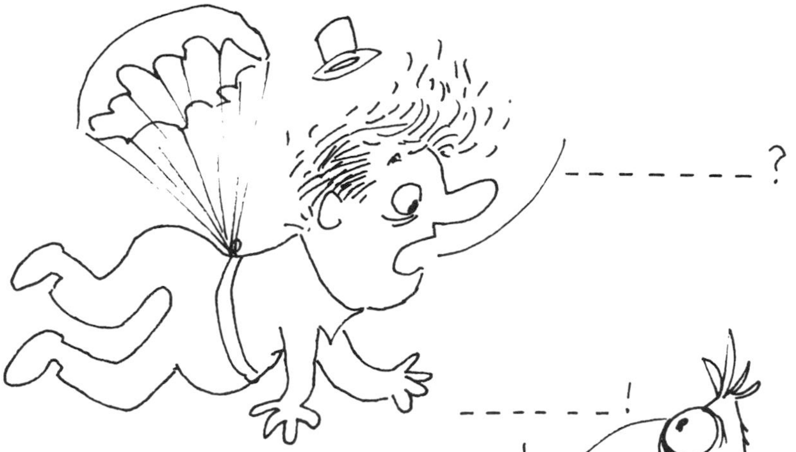

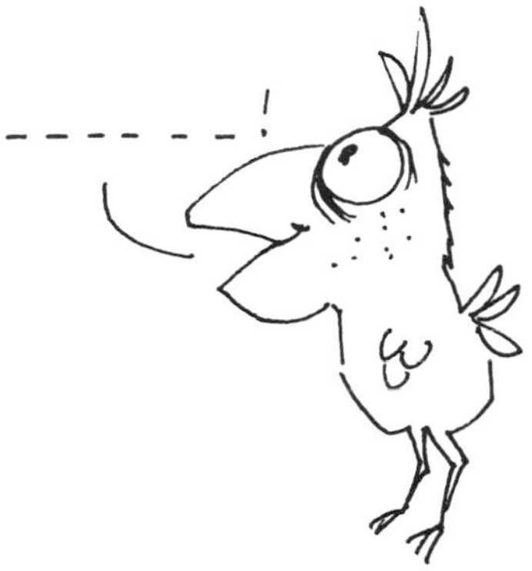

Sometimes a good cartoon can start with just the drawing. An odd or silly — or even crazy — drawing can suggest a gag. For example, look at the drawing below. It doesn't make any sense at all. But with a little thought you might be able to think of some conversation between the horse and the cowboy that would be funny. Or how about that parachutist in trouble? Starting with an unreal, peculiar event is halfway toward a complete cartoon.

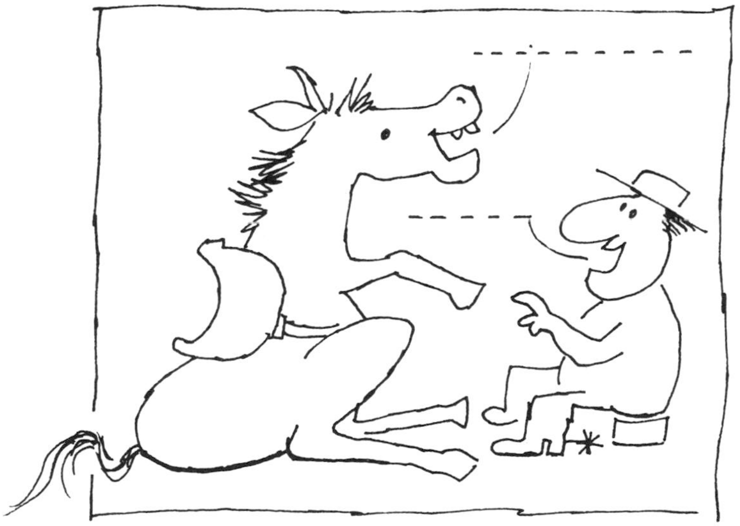

Some cartoons start out as conversation or as nonsense verse. For example, it wouldn't be hard to make a funny drawing using the verse: Rickey-Tickey poo,

My nose is stuck in glue!

Or, "Please sir, I'd like a fried egg ice cream cone," or "Does this bus use round or flat tires?" The sillier the better.

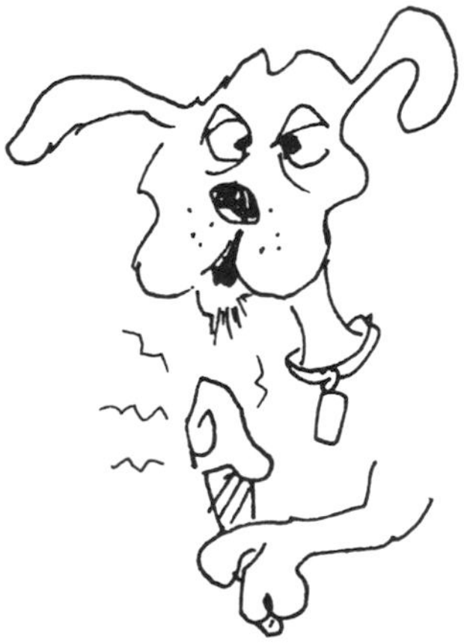

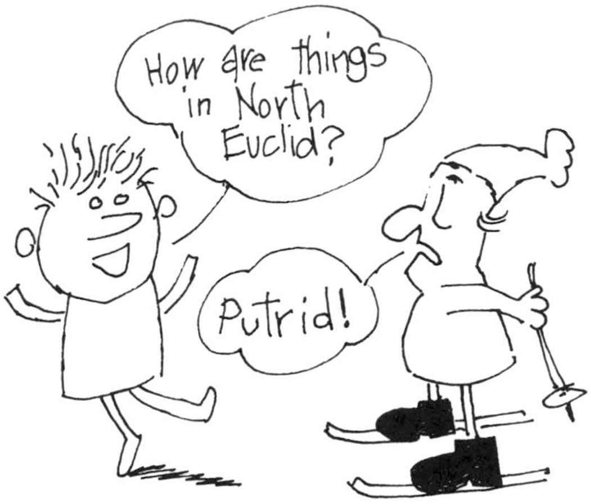
How are things in North Euclid?
Putrid!

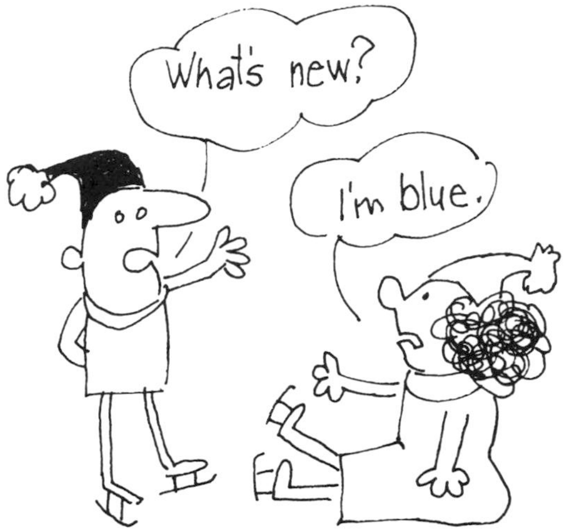
What's new?
I'm blue.

When cartoon characters are talking their words are often shown in balloons. The lettering is always done neatly and with care.▲

Sometimes conversation can be enlivened with dialect or odd kinds of speech. "Ohhh, deary me, but I iz somewhat doggone weary!" Dialect helps establish character and anyhow is fun to do. You can forget the rules of grammar and invent your own spelling.

When a drawing seems a bit ragged or spread out its appearance can often be improved with the use of a border.▼

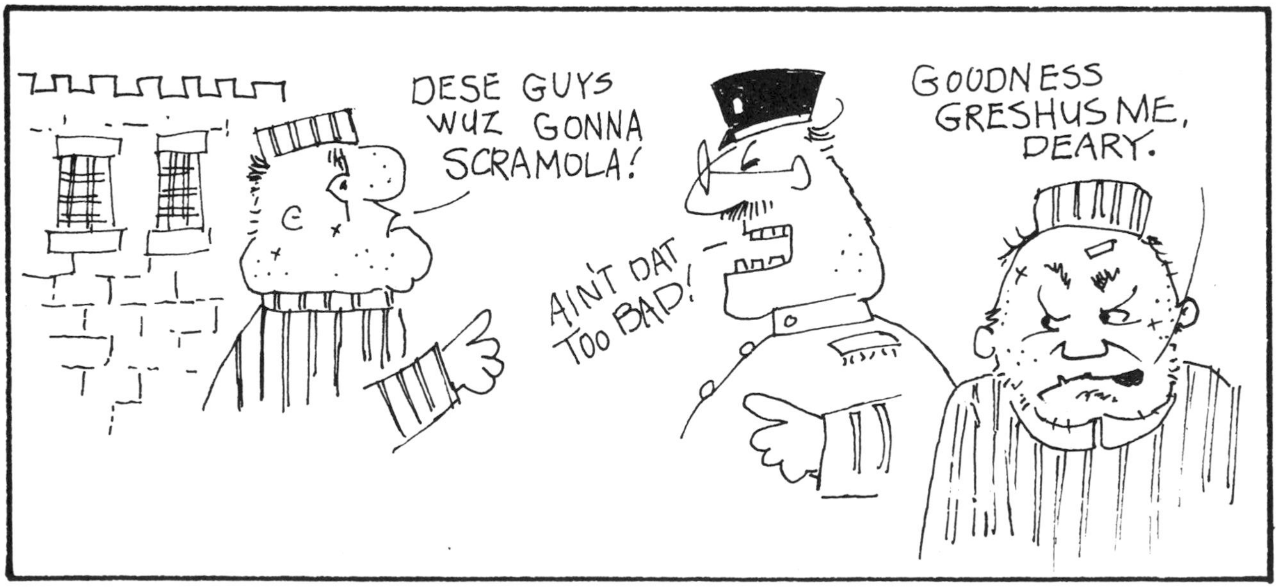
DESE GUYS WUZ GONNA SCRAMOLA!
AIN'T DAT TOO BAD!
GOODNESS GRESHUS ME, DEARY.

If you've made a cartoon or cartoon strip that you really like and want to give it to your friends or relatives it is an easy matter to get many copies by photocopying. This is a quite inexpensive way to get a lot of use out of one good idea.

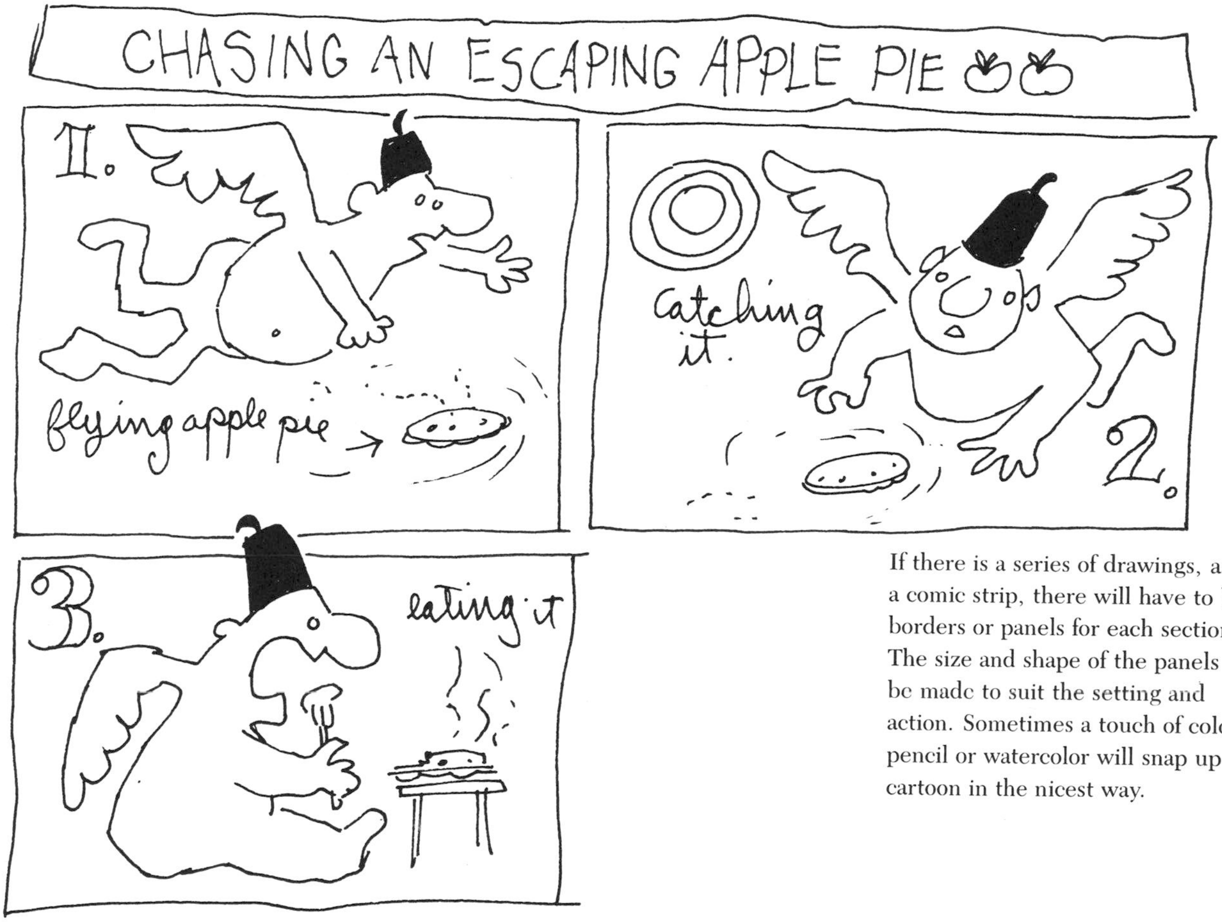
CHASING AN ESCAPING APPLE PIE
1.
flying apple pie
catching it.
2.
3.
eating it

If there is a series of drawings, as in a comic strip, there will have to be borders or panels for each section. The size and shape of the panels can be made to suit the setting and action. Sometimes a touch of colored pencil or watercolor will snap up a cartoon in the nicest way.

Many cartoonists get their ideas by looking at the work of other cartoonists and then changing what has already been done. This is not copying. It is letting one idea inspire another. You may find that a cartoon somewhere can start you off on something of your own . . . and you may very well decide that cartoons and cartooning are a very fine way to express some of your own humor, ideas, or opinions!

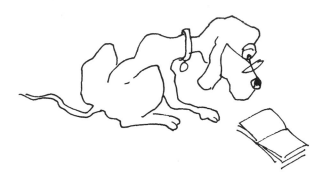

OTHER BOOKS

Many books about cartoons and cartooning may be found in your local library — collections of the work of a single cartoonist, cartoons from just one publication, or books that deal with only one cartoon character. There are histories of cartoonists from the distant past to the present. And there may be how-to-do-it books that will help you with your own drawing.

Here are a few books that you will find quite helpful . . .

Lexicon of Comicana by Mort Walker, Comicana, Inc.

How to Draw Comics the Marvel Way, Simon & Schuster.

Cartooning the Head and Figure, by Jack Hamm. A Perigree Book/Putnam Publishing.

The Smithsonian Collection of Newspaper Comics, edited by Bill Blackbeard and Martin Williams. Harry N. Abrams, Inc.

How to Draw and Sell Cartoons, by Ross Thomson and Bill Hewison, North Light.

Great Cartoonists and Their Art, by Art Wood, Pelican Publishing.